The Britannica
Story Book

Some First Facts for Early Learners

Prepared under the supervision of the editors of ENCYCLOPÆDIA BRITANNICA

The Britannica
Story Book

ENCYCLOPÆDIA BRITANNICA, INC.
Chicago

Auckland • Geneva • London • Manila • Paris • Rome • Seoul • Sydney • Tokyo • Toronto

AN INTRODUCTION TO
THE BRITANNICA STORY BOOK

The pages that follow in THE BRITANNICA STORY BOOK have been specifically designed for children from four to nine. The unusual diversity of art styles, the variety of writing forms and techniques, and the use of many comprehension levels are all part of a multilevel approach that assures the book's continued use in your home during the important years of your young child's growth.

Most children under ten are browsers. They rarely "look something up." Thus, no attempt has been made to be all-inclusive. Some subjects of particular interest to young children—hiccups, for instance— were selected in preference to more intellec-

tually significant topics because, in the judgment of the consultants and editors, they were better suited to colorful, lively treatment. The emphasis is on stimulating curiosity, on building concepts, and on opening doors into the universe, and not solely on the acquisition of facts. Inevitably, however, many facts will be absorbed as the articles are read and reread—and at different ages.

Professor Jerome S. Bruner of Harvard University has written, "Learning is so deeply ingrained in man that it is almost involuntary." As parents, you are particularly aware of the natural curiosity of children and of their desire to learn. Children are always asking "Why?" even though they usually are not asking for adult answers.

They ask questions about the world of things that grow and move. They ask about machines developed by people to make our lives easier (and often more complicated and frightening). They ask about outer space—the sun and the planets and the stars. And about mountains and rivers and

oceans. Our children want to know the whys and hows of so many things that we adults accept as commonplace.

In describing the ideas of Jean Piaget, one of the world's most famous psychologists, Dr. David Elkind, wrote, "Children . . . believe that everything has a purpose and that everything in the world is made by and for man." Dr. Elkind's five-year-old son, for example, once asked him why we have snow and then answered his own question by saying, "It's for children to play in."

Scientists have studied the process of conceptual learning for many years, and they are still debating the exact nature of this phenomenon. Many of their theories and discoveries were incorporated into the pages that follow. A team of writers, artists, editors, and educators spent many hours discussing what youngsters should find in a book like this. As you quickly look through it, you will see how these questions were resolved: sometimes with a silly jingle that makes an important point about under-

standing our feelings—and how to deal with them; sometimes with many pictures and very few words; sometimes with a fairy story from the past, or a modern story about boys and girls growing up in a complicated world; sometimes with humor.

There are articles about animals that tell how and why they live where they do. There is a story about why the ocean is salty and one about what it was like before there were automobiles. The child learns about making friends, bridges that move, and how a town starts. There is even an article that explains the difference between a storybook wolf and a real one.

A special caution is called for with respect to age ranges. Everyone knows how different a four-year-old is from a nine-year-old. Obviously, the same articles will not interest them both. But it is possible that a four-year-old will be fascinated by the illustrations for an article that is over his head in terms of subject treatment and writing level. And an eight-year-old may continue to read a catchy little poem intended for younger children, because she has discovered a dimension that even the editors missed.

Many children of twelve and older will tell their parents and teachers that they "aren't interested in books." And they are not. According to Dr. Bruner, "We get interested in what we get good at. In general, it is difficult to sustain interest in an activity unless one achieves some degree of competence." A poor reader will probably not like books. A child never exposed to books when he is young will probably not like them when he grows older. But his success in school and as a person will depend on his ability to read and comprehend. If, as your family uses THE BRITANNICA STORY BOOK, your youngsters are stimulated to seek out even one other book because their curiosity has been awakened, you will have truly succeeded in offering them a very special opportunity.

The Editors

The Man Who Told Animal Stories

Many, many years ago there was a man named Aesop who liked to tell stories about animals that acted very much the way some people do.

"A dog had a piece of meat in his mouth and was carrying it home. On the way he had to cross a stream. And as he looked into the water, he saw his reflection.

"Thinking that it was another dog with a piece of meat, he made up his mind to have that piece, too. So he snapped at the meat he saw in the water. As he opened his mouth, he dropped the real meat, and it was carried away by the stream.

"By being so greedy and trying to get more, the dog got nothing at all."

Another story was about a fox.

"Strolling through the woods one day, the fox saw a juicy bunch of grapes hanging from a high vine.

" 'Just the thing for a thirsty fox,' he said to himself.

"He jumped as high as he could to reach the grapes, but he missed. He tried again and again. Each time he just missed the tasty-looking fruit.

"Finally the fox quit trying.

" 'Oh, well,' he thought, 'those grapes are probably sour anyway.'

"And he went away without the grapes.

"*When the fox couldn't have what he wanted, he pretended he really didn't want it at all.*"

More than a hundred of the stories Aesop told have been written down. You can read them all in a book that you can get in almost any bookstore or library.

Animal Partners

Snap!

No, that's not the huge jaws of the crocodile clamping down on the little plover bird. It's the beak of the plover snatching food from between the wrinkles of the crocodile's thick skin.

In a way, the giant crocodile and the tiny bird are friends. They help each other. The bird picks off leeches and other bothersome water creatures that stick to the crocodile's skin. Sometimes the crocodile dozes with its frightful mouth open. Some people say the bird even goes inside its mouth to look for leeches or to pick food from between its teeth.

The bird pays the crocodile for its meals by squawking loudly when enemies are near, and the crocodile is warned.

The lizard and the bird called the *petrel* are friends, too. They even live together in a nest under the ground. The petrel builds the nest. The lizard keeps it clean by eating lice and other pests that keep creeping in.

Although the nest is not large, each has enough room to sleep. That's because the lizard stays at home and keeps house all day while the bird is out flying around. Then, when the bird wings its way home at night, the lizard goes out hunting.

A zebra and an ostrich—now there's a nice pair. Zebras and ostriches sometimes roam together. When they do, they have twice as much to eat and half as much to fear. This is because they take turns warning each other when danger is near.

On sunny days the ostrich, which can see much better and farther than the zebra, is the lookout, or scout.

On cloudy days or when it's growing dark, the zebra is the leader. The zebra hears better and has a sharper sense of smell than the ostrich. When it gets too dark to see, the zebra uses its ears and nose.

The big horn of an angry rhinoceros is one of the most dangerous weapons in the world. With its horn a rhinoceros can butt down a tree. It can protect itself from lions and tigers. Most people and creatures stay away from a rhinoceros—except for one little bird.

This bird is the rhino's partner. It is always welcome to perch on the rhino's back. That's because the bird sits there and eats the tiny insects that bite and bore into the hide of the great beast. The insects are called *ticks*. The bird is known as the *tickbird*.

So—because it hates the ticks that a tickbird likes—even the dangerous rhino has a friend.

One likes honey, and the other likes honeycomb.

The little bird called a *honey guide* flies high over the trees and bushes looking for a hive or a hollow tree where the bees keep their honey.

When the honey guide sees the hive, it turns and flies quickly to the ratel.

By chattering loudly from the air, the honey guide leads the ratel to the honeycomb.

Now it's time for the ratel to do its share of the work. It tears into the bees' nest with its strong, sharp claws. Its heavy, black-and-white fur protects it from the angry bees.

After the ratel has eaten its fill and scared some of the bees away, it's the honey guide's turn.

These are just a few of the creatures that help each other. Some are strong; some are weak. Some are fast; some are slow. Some are big; some are small. It is the ways in which they are different from each other that make it possible for them to help each other.

Before There Were Automobiles

The automobiles keep coming—too many to count. It's hard to imagine a street without them. And yet, there was a time when there were no automobiles anywhere.

Long, long ago, people had to walk wherever they wanted to go.
Later, men discovered that they could ride on the backs of
animals. Men rode camels, horses, donkeys, oxen, and elephants
on long trips. Long lines of camels—called *caravans*—carried
men and their belongings across the desert.

Then came the happy day when someone found out about wheels. How? No one is sure. But what a good thing it was when people learned to use wheels. Just try *rolling* a square block!

After they had wheels, people could carry things in carts and wagons. At first, people themselves pulled the carts. Later, animals —even dogs—were trained to do this.

At one time, carts called *chariots* were used by soldiers for fighting and racing.

Some people put sails on carts. The wind blew them along the ground, as it blows sailing ships across the water. Sailing carts

were fun but not very useful. If the wind blew very hard or took the cart over bumpy ground, the cart usually turned over!

One day somebody made a cart with pedals that could be pushed with the feet to make it go. The pedal cart became a *tricycle* when one wheel was removed. Taking a wheel off the tricycle made a two-wheeler—the first *bicycle*. Some people can even ride a "one-wheeler," called a *unicycle*.

People made bigger and bigger carts. In the United States great covered wagons creaked along, carrying people and supplies from one city to another. Stagecoaches pulled by four, and sometimes six, fast horses jounced and bounced as they rolled along the rough roads. Sometimes outlaws stopped the stagecoaches and robbed the passengers.

After the steam engine was invented, we had railroad trains. Now people could move *fast*! Trains rushed hundreds of people wherever the tracks went—and they went almost everywhere.

People started building better roads now, and they used steam engines instead of horses to move their carts. But before many steam carts were running on the roads, gasoline engines were invented. You know what we had then.

Automobiles!

Many people didn't like automobiles at first because sometimes horses were frightened by them and ran away. There were many horses then and not very many automobiles.

Things change. Things always keep changing. Today, there are not very many horses, but there are many automobiles!

Baby's First Year

My little brother, who just came,
Hasn't even got a name!
Look at his fingernails! So small
You hardly notice them at all.
Perhaps someday he'll learn to walk!
Perhaps someday he'll learn to talk!
But *now* all he can do is yell
And *that* he does *extremely* well.
Today my mommy said, "Once *you*
Were just like him."—And if that's true,
The chances are someday he'll be
A real live *person*—just like me.

On the day it's born, a baby bear could fit into your two hands. It's that tiny.

But by the time it's one year old, a bear cub is almost as big as the mother bear. It'll soon be ready to move out of the den that has been its home. It has learned the ways of grown-up bears.

By the time a cat or a dog is one year old, it's grown-up, too.

The very day it's born, a little colt can stand on its own legs. They're wobbly legs, and sometimes it tumbles—*oops!* But soon it knows all about walking.

The day *you* were born you couldn't do much except eat and sleep and cry. You couldn't even turn around by yourself.

You were bigger than a new bear cub, but you grew much more slowly.

For many years after they're born, children need to be taken care of by their mother and father.

At first, a baby can't move the way he really wants to. He kicks his feet and waves his hands in the air. But he can't do these things *on purpose*.

His head wobbles when he lifts it and then drops right down again. Months go by before the new baby is strong enough to hold up his head and look around. *Then* is he surprised!

It's a long time before baby starts reaching for things. At first he can only grab at something he wants to pick up or slap at it or play with it, much the way a kitten paws at a ball of yarn. But later baby discovers that he has *thumbs* as well as fingers and that he can pick up and hold things between his fingers and thumb.

Thumbs are very important to have. Try to pick up a pin, a ball, or a piece of string without using your thumb. Aren't you glad that your thumb is so handy—and that your hand is so thumby?

After learning what a fine thing a thumb is, each time baby touches Mommy's hair or Daddy's tie—or nose—he opens his fingers wide, closes them tight, and hangs on.

All this time baby is getting ready to walk. He wiggles and squirms, and then one day he rolls right over. *Waagh!* He may howl with rage and surprise the first time that happens. Soon, though, baby likes his new trick. And he likes the next one even better—being able to sit up without being held.

Then one day baby gets up on his hands and knees—and suddenly he's crawling! Now he can go from the chair to the table to the bookcase and can even pull himself up to stand. About the time he has his first birthday, he forgets to hang on to Mommy's hand and takes his first step alone.

Now baby can walk. He toddles and waddles from the kitchen to the bedroom to the front door. Sometimes he even tries to run. That's when he gets into trouble. It seems that he will never learn. But he's learning all the time. He just doesn't know he's learning. He finds out that chairs turn over, that dishes break, and that books can fall on his head.

Sometimes we call it mischief—but baby is just busy exploring. He moves, looks, and touches. He's like a puppy dog, poking and roaming and sniffing.

By now, baby is learning something else just as important as walking or using his thumbs and fingers. He is learning to *talk*.

All during his first year, baby has been making gurgles and chuckles and easy sounds like *da-da-da* or *ma-ma-ma*. His family is so happy when he says Mama that he says it again and again. He can understand some of the things his parents or brothers and sisters say to him now, especially no, no. He learns to say them, too.

By this time, a kitten has grown into a cat and probably has even had her own kittens. The young bear has learned to find its own food and can protect itself well enough to live alone. Baby can't do that. Not yet. He still has much growing and learning and exploring to do.

Can you remember when *you* learned to walk?

WALKING

I *think* I can remember back
   To when I couldn't walk at all,
And, just to get from here to there,
   I had to crawl and *crawl* and CRAWL.

The chairs, the chest of drawers, the desk
   All used to seem so far away!
They wouldn't even stir when I
   Invited them to come and play.

But then one day I took a step
   And then I took another one.
I learned to walk—and even more:
   To skip and hop and jump and run!

Biggest Family

A mother fish lays more eggs than you can count—often more than a million. She doesn't stay to take care of the baby fish that come from the eggs. After she drops her eggs in the water, she swims away.

When a baby fish comes out of one of the eggs, it has *hatched*. But not many of the eggs do hatch. Other fish—and frogs and turtles—eat many of the fish eggs. Some of the eggs float onto the land, where birds eat them.

A mother bird usually lays only as many eggs as can be kept warm with her body—usually four or five eggs. After they're hatched, she feeds and protects the baby birds and helps them learn to fly.

Very large animals, such as horses and cows and elephants, almost always have only one baby at a time.

But small animals, such as mice and rabbits and opossums, have several babies at a time.

A mother hamster can have as many as 12 babies—a dozen— about every month. And in just a few weeks, those babies can start having babies of their own—often every month!

In countries where hamsters are wild, the owls and foxes and wolves hunt them, so not many of the hamsters grow up. If they did, then, beginning with just one pair of hamsters, more than one million hamsters could be running around by the end of a year.

Boys and girls are almost always born one at a time.

When they're born two at a time, they're called *twins*.

When they're born three at a time, they're called *triplets*.

When they're born four at a time, they're called *quadruplets*.

Once in a great, great while they're born five at a time, and then they're called *quintuplets*.

Babies grow slowly, and they grow for a long time. And during all this time their parents take care of them and keep them safe and try to help them grow up happily.

It takes a long time before a human family can grow this big.

Tim Says

My brother Tim, who's now eleven,
　Began to read when he was seven.
I'm only six—but soon, says Tim,
　I shall be reading just like him.

If you know where, says Tim, to look,
　You're always bound to find a book
That tells you almost instantly
　—No matter what the thing may be—
Exactly what you want to know.
　Why does it rain? Why does it snow?
Find out, says Tim, in books on science.
　And Tim says other books have giants;
And some have elves and wicked witches,
　Magic lamps and buried riches.
In one a boy named Tom was brave
　Till he was rescued from a cave.

Tim says he's read a hundred tales
　Of animals, from mice to whales;
Of horses flying through the sky;
　Of little men six inches high;
Cannibals and Indian scouts;
　Great victories or bloody routs
In battles long ago; or fights
　On horseback between armored knights.

The books are waiting on the shelf.
　"Soon you'll be reading them yourself,"
Says Tim; and what Tim says is so.
　Look out, books! Here I come! Let's go!

Bridges That Move

All bridges are built because someone
who is *here*   wants to be   *there*.

The castle drawbridge was built so that only friends could
cross from

here   to   *there*, or from
there   to   *here*.

A lookout in the high tower warned when enemies were near.
Then the castle folk hurried to pull one end of the bridge all the
way up. Road closed! No bridge!

The idea of building bridges that could be raised or moved was so good that it is still used today.

When a tall ship approaches, the two halves of this drawbridge are pulled up. The cars on both sides must stop to let the ship sail through.

All drawbridges are not alike. Some rise at one end,

others turn to make way for the ship,

and some rise straight up, like an elevator.

Bridges make it easier for people—whether walking or driving or riding in trains—to get where they want to go.

What Is a Castle?

Long ago, one of the safest places you could be in was a castle. It was a fort to keep out robbers, fierce armies, wild animals, and harsh weather.

Castles have a magical look, which makes it easy to believe everything you read in fairy tales about the wizards and giants and wicked queens who built castles in the twinkling of an eye.

Long ago—about a thousand years ago—great lords really *did* build castles to live in. (Lords were rich and powerful men who were supposed to protect the people called *serfs,* who worked and fought for them.) The lord also used his castle as a fort when he had to battle enemy lords. Some greedy lords wanted to capture as many castles as they could.

It is a wonder that castles were ever built at all. Most of them were made so long ago that every single job had to be done by hand. There were almost no machines—no bulldozers for digging, no giant cranes or steam shovels for lifting, no trucks for hauling.

Instead, there were hundreds and hundreds of men to do the work—

carpenters to saw and fit the wood

workers to hammer and bend the metals

workers to cut and place the stone

and cooks to feed everybody.

If you were a great lord who had enough money to build a castle, where would you begin?

First, you would think about which part of your land would be easiest to keep safe from the enemy and which part would be easiest for enemy lords to take away from you.

Would you build your castle at the bottom of a hill—or at the top?

Suppose your land lay along a river. Would you choose a straight part of the river or a place where the river curved?

You're right—a high, rocky place on the bend of a river would probably be best.

You would gather all your building materials and prepare places for your workmen to live for as long as three or four years. Then you would be ready to build.

First you would build a high stone wall around the place where your castle was going to be. Along the top of this wall there would be places to shoot arrows from and places to hide behind in battles.

At the corners of the walls you would build towers. If the towers were round, ladders could not easily be used to climb them. If the towers were pointed, stones would roll right off them and fall back down on the enemy.

The largest and strongest tower, which you would build inside the wall, would be the *keep*, where the lords and ladies would live and be "kept" safe.

If you had to build your castle on flat ground, your men would dig a wide *moat*, or ditch, all around the outside of the wall. It would be connected to the river so that it could be filled with water. You would have your carpenters make a drawbridge across the moat and a bridge tower to protect it. Then your workers would make a gate for the bridge that could be closed and locked very tightly.

You would have to build your castle big enough so that in it you would have these places and more—

a Great Hall for eating and meeting,

a kitchen for cooking,

a chapel for prayers,

a jail below ground for prisoners, called the *dungeon;*

and don't forget a place for soldiers to live

and a place for dogs and also for the horses, which served as cars and trains and planes do today.

Well, there you have your castle.

If you have building blocks or even dominoes, you can build a pretty good castle of your own. Try it.

The Tiger in Your House

Is this a wild jungle tiger about to jump out of the page and eat somebody?

No. It is a cuddly, soft kitten playing in someone's house.

But a tiger is a cat. So is a lion, a leopard, a cheetah, a jaguar, a lynx, a panther, and a puma. They are all cats.

All of them leap and run and pounce and snarl.

Many climb trees.

Many purr and meow.

Many don't like to go in water.

They can see better at night than people can.

They are among the fastest of furred animals.

They have five toes on their front paws and four on their back paws. And probably you have found out that cats have long, sharp claws. They use their claws for climbing trees, catching food, and protecting themselves against other animals. The claws in the front toes of most cats can be moved in and out. Now you see them, and now you don't.

Yes, your soft, playful kitty and the lion, leopard, and tiger are all cats. But not all cats are pet cats. Not all cats are the kind of cats you would want to put your arms around and cuddle.

A new baby lion is so small that you could hold it in your arms. But lions grow very fast. A baby lion would soon be big enough to hold *you* in its arms.

There have been cats on the Earth for a very, very long time. Much longer than dogs and wolves and bears.

As far back as caveman days, there were wildcats prowling the woods. Cavemen probably tamed some of the smaller cats and let them live in the caves, where they could chase away the rats and mice and snakes that tried to get in.

One cat called the *saber-toothed tiger* was *not* a pet. It was as big as some automobiles of today. Cavemen scared these cats away with fires they kept burning at night.

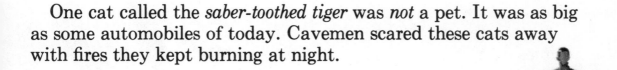

Long ago in the country of Egypt, the people thought that cats were magic. The Egyptian people made statues of cats out of wood and stone. Milk for the cats was sometimes put in saucers of gold. When cats died, they were buried in special cat graveyards.

In another country—once called Siam—cats lived in the castles with the kings. Some cats were trained to be warrior cats and to guard the castle walls. Siamese cats have very loud voices. They were supposed to yowl and screech a warning if enemies came near.

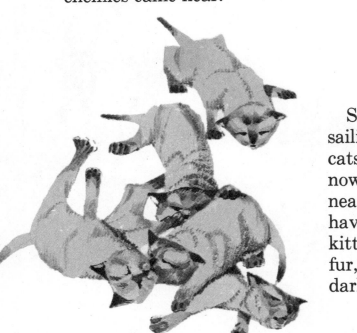

Sea captains of the old-time sailing ships brought Siamese cats home to their children, and now these blue-eyed cats are nearly everywhere. Perhaps you have seen them. When they are kittens, they have soft, white fur, with a dark nose and tail and dark ears and paws.

Today for pets we have short-haired cats and long-haired cats, as well as bobtail, calico, Maltese, tiger, tabby, and many other kinds of cats. Cats are among the smartest of all tame animals. They can do tricks— open doors and ring doorbells. But lots of times they don't want to. It is hard to teach them tricks, because they don't like to be bossed. They like to have their own way.

You may have heard people say that cats have nine lives. They don't, really. But they are so quick and so surefooted that they may escape danger many times in their lives.

How A Clown Makes His Face

When is a clown not a clown?

He *is* a clown when he's performing at the circus—wearing huge floppy shoes, baggy clothes, and a funny face. And he's a clown when he's riding on a tiny tricycle or walking on skinny stilts or chasing another clown. Sometimes he does dangerous tricks on a high wire. But he's still a clown.

When is a clown not a clown? When he's just an ordinary man—before the show. Before he puts on his clown costume and paints on his own special clown face.

Let's go into his dressing room and see him change from an ordinary man into a clown.

First his jacket and tie come off . . . and a smock goes on. Clown makeup is messy.

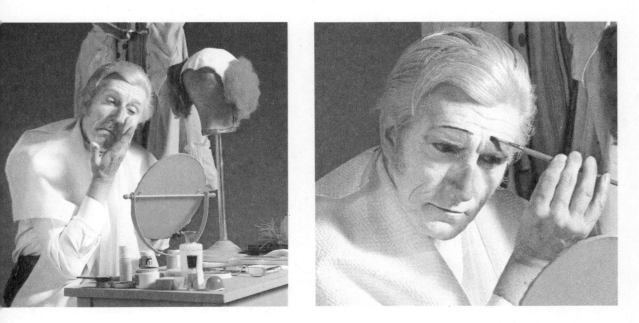

The white paint is so thick that it looks as if he's wearing a mask, and so greasy that it's called *greasepaint*. A smear of red on his nose. Blue above his eyes. Thick, black eyebrows high above where they belong.

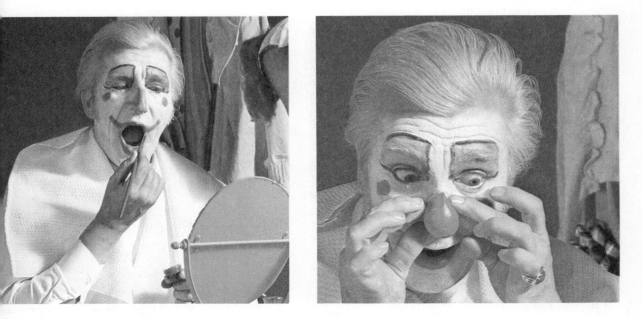

A bright red spot for each cheek. A smear of red that covers his lips and makes his smile twice as wide as it really is. A nose as round and as red as a plum.

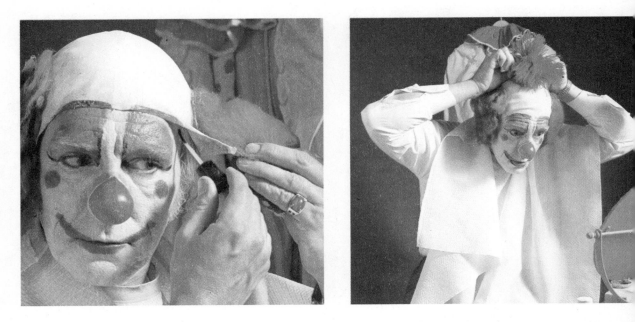

A tight-fitting cap that covers his hair has funny, green hair of its own. Add a topper of red feathers.

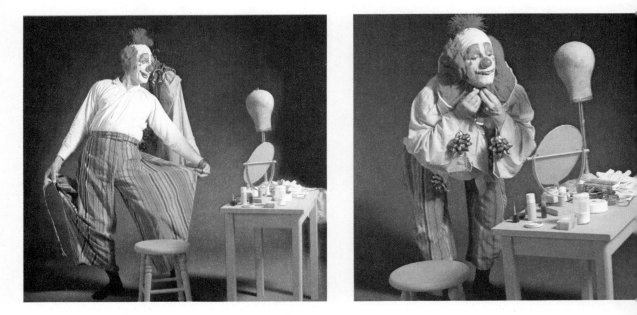

The big, baggy pantaloons make even the clown laugh. On with the shirt and a funny, ruffly collar.

Tying his shoes can be a BIG problem!

Just in case it should rain . . .

Hurry! Hurry! The show's about to begin.
And here comes the clown, bouncing and
dancing and looking like no other clown
in the world. Because each clown owns
his own clown face, and no other clown
in the world is supposed to use it.

Builders in the Sea

How can a tiny sea creature make a wall big enough to wreck a ship?

It doesn't make the wall by itself—it has help from many other tiny coral creatures. Together they make this great seawall, or *reef*.

What is *coral?*

Coral is a soft, little animal that looks like a bit of jelly. And the hard, little shell houses that the soft, little animals live in are called coral, too.

People sometimes make jewelry from chunks of the coral wall.

Under the ocean where the water is warm, coral grows in lovely ocean gardens. It grows in just about every color and shape you can think of. It may grow to look like lace, a fan, a leaf, the horns of a deer. Or it may grow together in a reef a hundred miles long.

No matter what coral grows to look like, it starts as a tiny, soft animal not so big as the end of your little finger. The baby coral swims through the water until it finds a place to build its house, and then it never swims again.

Using a special glue from inside its body, it sticks itself to a rock or to another piece of coral.

Once it is stuck, it starts to build itself a house. It builds the house with a juice that comes out of its body and turns into a kind of stone.

But if it never goes outside its house, how does the coral eat?

It pokes long feelers through a tiny door in its house. The feelers wave around in the water. When they touch a tiny plant or animal floating nearby, the feelers pull this food inside the house for the coral to eat.

One day a bud grows on the coral. The bud grows into a new coral animal, which builds a house around itself so much like the first coral's house you couldn't tell them apart.

After many years, there are so many coral houses built on top of one another and next to each other that the coral may grow into a great stone wall.

The ocean waves wash sand between the coral reefs. Trees may start to grow in the sand. Now the coral is part of an island where people can live. Maybe airplanes will land on the island. People on ships may visit it to buy coconuts.

It seems that coral might keep on growing until it filled the ocean. But the coral has enemies. Fish bite through the little stone house and eat the soft coral living inside. Worms and snails drill holes through the coral's house. And sometimes, when the waves are very rough and strong, big pieces of coral are broken off.

But more coral always keeps growing.

Pterodactyl

Brontosaur

Stegosaur

Monsters of the Past

They were the biggest, scariest creatures that ever lived. The word *dinosaur* means "terrible lizard." Which one of these do you think was the most terrible?

Brontosaur. The "thunder lizard" weighed as much as ten elephants and probably sounded like thunder when it walked. But it ate only plants—never touched a bit of meat.

Pterodactyl. It'd even scare a witch on a broomstick! This "wing-fingered" dinosaur swooped across the sky like a dragon kite.

Tyrannosaur

Trachodon

Triceratops

Stegosaur. This one was covered with hard, bony plates from head to tail. And when it wagged that tail, it wasn't being friendly. The tail had four long spikes at the tip.

Tyrannosaur. This dinosaur, known as the "king of the lizards," was as long as a fire truck. The teeth in its jaws were like big knives.

Trachodon. This terrible duck-billed lizard had 2,000 teeth!

Triceratops. This "three-horned" lizard looked like an army tank and was just as unfriendly.

There were many other kinds of dinosaurs. They lived almost everywhere. The very land beneath your bedroom may once have throbbed and thundered to the tread of these huge creatures.

What if dinosaurs were still alive?

How impatient you'd be if a dinosaur were in your way as you tried to cross the street!

How surprised you'd be if you awoke one night to see a dinosaur peering in your upstairs bedroom window!

How little food there'd be for you to eat if you had to share it with a dinosaur! Some of them ate more food in *one day* than you eat in a whole year.

You don't have to worry about any of this happening, of course, because dinosaurs completely disappeared from the Earth so long ago that it is hard to think back that far.

How do we know that once upon a time there were dinosaurs? Because we keep finding their bones.

Let's pretend we are living in dinosaur days, when the air was hot and thick and heavy, and there was water here and there and everywhere because it rained so much. And here we are, hidden behind the leaves of the topmost branch of a tree that grows by a muddy pond. We see that the enormous log near the edge of the pond is not a log at all. It is a duck-billed dinosaur that has been taking a nap. Now it's getting up! It's clambering out of the water and heading toward our tree!

The duckbill rips the leaves from a branch that's almost touching the one on which we're hiding. Now it lowers its head, munching the leaves. It swallows them in one gulp. *Rip!* There go the leaves on a branch that's even closer to us.

Suddenly, high above the treetops, we see the head of a dinosaur that is even taller and uglier than the first one. We know from its great size and the hooklike claws on its short front feet that this is the kind of dinosaur called "king of the lizards," the most dangerous beast on Earth.

Its mouth opens and closes like a giant pair of scissors. Terrible cries tear across the sky as the "king of the lizards" starts after the duckbill. When the fight is over, the duck-billed dinosaur is dead. After eating as much of the duckbill as it can, the lizard king waddles away to find a quiet place to sleep until it is hungry again.

The bones of the duckbill lie at the edge of the pond.

It begins to rain, and the rain washes the bones over the edge of the pond into the water.

More rains come and wash dirt from the bank of the pond. The dirt settles as mud over the bones. This happens for millions of years.

Slowly, as millions of more years go by, the weather changes. There is little or no rain. The sun shines hot. It shines everywhere because there is no shade. The grass and trees have dried up and blown away in hot winds. The mud that surrounded the duckbill bones is dry now, too, and nearly as hard as rock. The duckbill is buried under an almost empty desert.

Who knows? Maybe nobody will ever find its bones. But maybe they will. Some day an explorer (maybe you!) might come along, looking for dinosaur bones. He might dig in just the right place and find them. What a wonderful discovery!

It has happened before. It has happened many times. And today in the museums of big cities, you can see these bones put together as they were when they were part of real dinosaurs many millions of years ago.

They Swim Like Fish

Splish! Splash!
A whistle blows, and slick, shining gray creatures swim around and around in the big tank. Faster and faster. And then . . .

They leap out of the water. Up, up, up into the sunlit air. For a moment the great gray creatures are like birds flying. One after the other they leap up to snatch fish from the hand of their trainer, who is standing on a high platform.

The show is on! And it's one of the most amazing animal shows you could ever see.

Dolphins live in water and swim with fins. They look like fish. They swim like fish.

But they aren't fish. They're whales. Small whales. (You can see how a *big* whale looks swimming next to a dolphin!)

Dolphins need to stick their heads out of water to breathe. Otherwise they would drown. They even have a special hole on top of their heads for blowing air in and out.

The dolphin you see at the bottom of this page has a funny name—bottle-nosed dolphin. That's because its nose is shaped like the neck of a bottle.

And now . . . on with the show.

The trainer tosses rubber rings out over the water in the tank. The dolphins seem to dance back and forth on their tails as they jump through the whirling hoops.

Then there might be a basketball game, with the dolphins bumping balls into a basket with their rubbery heads. The show ends when they catch silly hats to wear over their beaklike noses.

The friendly, playful dolphins look as if they're having as much fun as the people watching them.

You might think that dolphins are most at home in water tanks. But their real home is in the ocean.

It would be strange to see a dolphin swimming by itself. Dolphins travel together—sliding down the waves made by ships (like a toboggan ride) or rolling on their sides in the foam.

Dolphins are kind to each other and to people. There are many stories of dolphins using their heads to bump swimmers in trouble to the shore. And if they see an injured dolphin under the water, they sometimes nudge it to the top so that it can get air to breathe.

There is only one creature that the dolphin has been known to attack—the shark. And that is just about the fiercest fish of all. A group of angry dolphins will ram their heads at a shark until the shark is killed or swims away.

One of the many amazing things a dolphin can do is to make "talking" sounds. They make more different sounds than any other animals except people.

Dolphins whistle, bark, squawk, squeak, and make clicking sounds. Most people who have studied dolphins believe that each sound means something different. Dolphins use a certain kind of whistle when they are frightened. They make other sounds when they are hungry or angry or just playful.

Some scientists think that dolphins are "talking" to each other in their own special way when they make these sounds. No one knows for sure. But we do know that dolphins can learn all kinds of difficult tricks. They are very, very intelligent—perhaps among the most intelligent creatures on Earth.

Someday, someone might prove that dolphins are having real conversations. Just like people—only with dolphin sounds.

A dolphin that I met today
Spoke to me in the strangest way.
Were those words I heard him speak?
Or was it just a friendly squeak?
What do you think?

The Donkey's Shadow

One hot summer's day a young man hired a donkey and a driver to take him to the next town. Carrying the young man, the donkey trudged along the dusty road, while the driver walked ahead.

The afternoon sun became so hot that the young man told the driver to stop. The only shade was the donkey's shadow, and so the man settled himself there.

But the driver said, "Wait! *I* want to sit there."

"Didn't I hire the donkey for the whole trip?" asked the young man. "There isn't enough shade for both of us."

"Yes, you hired the donkey," the driver said, "but you certainly said nothing about hiring its shadow."

And as they stood in the road and argued, the donkey kicked up its heels and ran away, taking its shadow with it.

A Special School

In the country of Burma in Asia there are many little one-room schoolhouses. They hold only one pupil at a time.

On the first day of school a wrinkled old teacher stands at the gate waiting for the pupil to arrive.

The pupil is only five years old. He is brought to school by teen-age boys. But he doesn't go in at once.

He is not sure he wants an education.

The teacher helps him make up his mind by shoving him into the schoolhouse from behind. Then the boys close the gate.

Now the pupil is sure he doesn't want an education! He starts to howl.

The boys gather around, offering him bananas and sweets. The pupil is very fond of eating, so he stops howling now and then to take a banana. Finally, after many bananas, he decides that school isn't so bad. Perhaps he will stay.

What kind of school is this?

It is a school for little Indian elephants. The wrinkled, old teacher is a wrinkled old elephant about 50 years old called a *koonkie*. The boys or men who help to train the little elephant are elephant riders. They are called *oozies*.

One oozie will become the little elephant's own driver and will stay with him all his life if he can.

What does the little elephant learn in school?

After a great deal of fussing around, and after pounds and pounds of bananas, he learns to let the oozie sit on his head. He learns the meaning of a few words, such as "Sit down!" and "Stand up!" But mostly he learns touch signals. If the oozie touches him on the ear or leans forward or backward, the elephant knows he is to go faster or slower or to stop or to kneel.

If the elephant is trained with kindness and patience, if he is praised and fussed over and given many treats, he will learn quickly. When he is older, he will work in a forest, dragging heavy logs or pulling up trees.

There are two kinds of elephants, Indian and African. Indian elephants are somewhat smaller than the African, and because they are gentler, many of them are trained to work for man. Most of the elephants we see in zoos or doing tricks in circuses are Indian.

Wild elephants live in herds in the forests of southeastern Asia. They are fairly easy to capture.

First, men build a strong pen.

Then some men called *beaters*, carrying drums and horns and clappers and gongs, get behind a herd of elephants. They make such a racket beating their drums and gongs that they scare and confuse the elephants. The elephants run away from the noise and right into the pen.

Of course, they don't like it at first. But if they are treated kindly, in time they are willing to learn, just as the little elephant was.

African elephants are larger and stronger than the Indian elephants. They have bigger ears and thicker skin. They get to be more than 11 feet tall—about twice as tall as a man. They weigh more than 12,000 pounds—as much as a school bus weighs! They are the largest animals that walk on land—the only animals in the world that are larger are whales.

Elephants used to live in many places in Africa, but so many were killed by hunters for their valuable ivory tusks that there are not so many left anymore.

Male elephants have huge tusks from six to nine feet long. They use them for digging up roots to eat and for carrying things and, if necessary, for fighting.

But elephants don't fight much. Except for man, they have no enemies. They are so big that no other animals attack them. And they don't attack or eat other animals.

They eat leaves and bark and fruits and nuts and vegetables.

They travel in herds, following a leader, and are always looking for a good place to have a picnic. When they find a nice, little grove of trees, they have dinner. They break the branches off the trees to eat the leaves as we would break off a stalk of celery. Sometimes they just butt with their heads and knock down a whole tree.

Baby elephants shuffle along with a traveling herd, hanging onto their mothers' tails with their trunks. The mothers take good care of their babies. Sometimes they even "plaster" them with mud. Does a mother elephant know that this gives her baby some protection against insect bites and stings? It seems so. All the elephants keep an eye on the babies, for they are the pets of the herd.

If an elephant happens to be sick or hurt, the other elephants take care of it, too. They never go on and leave it behind.

Elephants don't like the heat, and during the hot part of the day, they might take a nap. The older elephants sleep standing up, but the babies lie down and stretch out.

Elephants like to swim. When they come to a river, they wade in to cool off. They splash and squirt each other and give each other showers. On their backs, the babies sometimes slide down mudbanks. They all have a wonderful time.

A very special thing about an elephant is its trunk.

It's about six feet long and made up of strong, easily bending muscles.

The elephant breathes through its trunk and smells with it, so it is something like a nose.

He picks up food and heavy weights with it, so it is something like an arm.

He picks up tiny nuts and blades of grass with it, so it is something like a hand.

He makes loud noises with it, so it is something like a horn.

He sucks water up in it and gives himself a shower, so it is something like a garden hose.

When he swims underwater, he sticks it up in the air like a snorkel and breathes through it.

Mother elephants stroke and cuddle their babies with it.

And elephant sweethearts link trunks and walk off into the forest together.

Do You Want to Be an Explorer?

Maybe you want to know what's on the next street,
or in a cave,
or on an island where nobody lives,
or even in a locked closet in your own house.

Especially a locked closet!

If so, you know how an explorer feels.

Explorers are people who go to faraway places to find out what is there. They sail across oceans, climb mountains, and cut their way through forests where snakes and wild animals live.

Sometimes they become lost in icy blizzards, in hot and dry deserts, or in dark forests. Often they are hungry and thirsty and tired.

Then why do they go exploring?

Long ago—very, very long ago—
when there were no machines
in the world and everybody lived
in trees or caves, people went
exploring to find food and water.

After people learned how to
build houses, they went exploring
for other reasons, too. Some went
to look for gold and jewels and
furs and spices. Some went to find
new lands for their king or queen.
Some went to find slaves to do
their work for them. Some tried
to find a new way to get to the
other side of the world.

Perhaps the best reason of all
for people to go exploring is that
they are curious and want to go
somewhere new. Many men have
wanted to know what it was like
in some faraway place.

An explorer named Ferdinand
Magellan and his sailors left
Spain and sailed toward the set-
ting sun to see how far they
could go. After sailing week after
week on the ocean, they ran out
of food. They became so hungry
that they ate sawdust and
leather.

One of the sailors told of "great
and awful things of the ocean"—ugly flying fish, sharks, sea lions,
giant crabs, and fearful sea serpents.

Finally, they sighted an
unknown land. Their ships sailed
through a narrow path, or
channel, of stormy water between
high mountains and came to
another ocean—the biggest ocean
in the world. Magellan named it
the Pacific Ocean, and the channel where his ships sailed was
named the Strait of Magellan.

One of Magellan's ships was
the first to sail all the way
around the world.

In the mountains of Mexico an explorer named Cortés discovered the land of the Aztec Indians. It was like discovering a new world. Some of the Aztec houses were on floating islands in a lake. Many houses were almost buried in flowers.

Strange buildings—pyramids made of stones—pointed high into the sky. Around the pyramids for many miles was a tall new plant, green and waving in the wind. Some of the explorers had never seen it before. They didn't know what it was.

Corn! The tall, green, waving plant was corn.

The Aztecs also had gold—a lot of gold. The explorers knew what that was. Some explorers were cruel and greedy people. They fought the Indians and took their gold.

"I will find a way or make one," said Robert E. Peary.

Peary wanted to be first to reach the North Pole—a faraway place of ice and snow where it is light day and night in the middle of the summer and dark day and night in the middle of the winter.

Peary learned that explorers must be patient, as well as brave. He broke his leg and had to wait. He froze his toes and had to wait again. Storms and icy fog and polar bears caused more waiting. The sunlit snow almost blinded him. Some of his men died, and others turned back.

Only one man who had started out with him, Matthew Henson, was still with him when, finally, he reached the North Pole.

Look on the globe. You'll see
the South Pole, as well as the
North Pole. Both are places of
icy blizzards and are very cold.
With snowshoes and dog teams,
a man named Amundsen raced a
man named Scott to be the first
one to the South Pole. Amundsen
was first. Scott reached it soon
afterward, but he was so weak
from hunger and cold that he
died on the way home.

The first man to fly an airplane
over both the North Pole and
the South Pole was Admiral Byrd.

Today in an airplane an explorer can go farther in a minute
than a dog team sometimes went in a whole day. And today, radio
keeps explorers in touch with the rest of the world.

Do you like to read about faraway, hard-to-reach places? You
can because of books about explorers who dared to go to these
places. Now most of the land on the Earth has been explored. But
the bottoms of the oceans haven't—or not very much. And
today's explorers are just beginning to explore space. There will
always be something new to be curious about.

Exploring with Animals

Boats, airplanes, automobiles, and tractors can take explorers *almost* everywhere they want to go.

But in mountains high and rocky, through swamps low and sloppy, across deserts dry and dusty, over snow deep and crusty, explorers need animals to help them explore.

If you went exploring, what kind of animal would you choose to carry your food and tools and tent—and to carry you, too?

Would you choose a horse?

Many explorers do go exploring with horses. But some other animals are even better for exploring special places. One of these is the donkey.

Donkeys look much like horses, but they are smaller—except for their ears, which are longer. Donkeys almost never slip or trip, and they can carry heavy loads on narrow, rocky mountain trails.

Another good partner for an explorer is the mule. A mule's mother is a horse. A mule's father is a donkey. And a mule is big and strong like a horse, and patient and surefooted like a donkey. Mules do not become frightened at lightning or thunder. They do not even run away if bullets are banging or if rocks are rolling under their hooves on a mountain trail.

Another surefooted traveler is the llama. Llamas have shaggy coats and can carry loads over high mountains. But when a llama gets tired, it sits down and rests. Don't try to make it get up and go before it is ready. It might spit right in your eye!

What if you came to a *swamp* when you were exploring? A swamp is a sticky, oozy, glubby mud-and-water place that looks and feels like a giant mud pie.

A good animal partner for you in a swamp would be a water buffalo. This big animal looks something like a cow. It can wade through mud to the top of its legs.

An elephant is another animal that can wade with a heavy load on its back through a swamp. An elephant is the biggest land animal in the world. It is so strong that it can butt through the thick trees and vines of a jungle where there is no road at all.

A *desert* is as different from a swamp as anything could be. A swamp has too much water. A desert doesn't have enough. To explore in a dry, sandy desert, you would need an animal partner with feet like soft bouncy cushions. These help it walk across the sand without sinking into it. Your animal partner in a desert should also be one that can travel a long time without drinking any water, because water is hard to find there.

What you would need in a desert is a camel.

Suppose you wanted to go exploring in the far, cold Northland. A reindeer would be a good partner. It can pull a heavy sled over snow and ice.

Eskimo dogs also pull sleds. Some Eskimo dogs look like wolves and are almost as wild as wolves, but they can be harnessed like horses.

In the highlands of Asia lives another good traveling companion—the yak. Yaks have long, shaggy, black coats and long curving horns. They look a *little* like buffalo. They can travel comfortably on high, twisting mountain trails, in winds that are as cold and sharp as icicles. If you went exploring in the high, cold mountains, you might want to ride on the back of a yak.

Here are a few rhymes about a traveling yak.
Maybe you would like to make up a rhyme of
your own.

On a twisting trail
With a pack on his back,
A yak set out on a narrow track.
The track was so crooked, alas and alack,
The shaggy yak met himself—coming back.

A yak
With a pack
On his shaggy back
Went for a walk
On the railroad track.
The train came scurrying, *clickety-clack,*
And bumped the yak with a pack on his back.

Traveling a trail
With a pack on his back,
A yak named Jack
Met a yak named Mack.
Said the yak named Jack
To the yak named Mack,
"Get off of this track
Or I'll give you a whack!"
Said the yak named Mack
To the yak named Jack,
"You shaggy old yak,
Go sit on a tack!"

Finding New Friends

In this airplane, Rita and her family flew over the ocean. Now their long trip has ended. They have reached a new country— Canada—one they have never lived in or visited before.

People often move to a new home or neighborhood. Some families travel by car or train or boat to live in new cities. And some families, such as Rita's, even move a long, long way because they have heard good things about how they can live in a new country.

Rita thinks to herself, "In my new home I will have a room of my own. I will have many friends. I will like it here."

Then why is Rita crying?

When Rita is happy, her eyes shine as if they had little suns in them. But now she's crying, and that's because she can't find her big brother. She has looked all over the playground, but Juan is not there.

If you have a big brother and he goes to the same school, do you cry when you can't find him? Probably not. Because if he is like most big brothers, he just makes a funny face or teases you when he sees you and then runs away to play with the other big boys.

But if you had just moved to a large city in Canada from a little town in Puerto Rico . . .

If you didn't understand what people were saying, and if people didn't understand what you were saying—if everyone spoke English, and you spoke only Spanish except for a few words like *hello* and *good-bye* and *okay* . . .

And if nobody wanted you to be on his side . . .

Then your big brother would know how lonely and homesick you were, and he would not tease you.

Juan didn't tease his sister when—finally—they met on the playground.

He talked to her in their own language.

"I just found out how to play that game!"

Rita stopped crying and listened while he explained.

"*Bueno!* Good!" She had played that game in Puerto Rico. Now it was easy to guess what those English-speaking children were saying. She watched anxiously while Juan went over to them. Juan had studied English before the family had left Puerto Rico. Now he asked the children if Rita could play in their game.

"My sister knows the rules," he said, "and she can run very fast."

The leader of one of the teams said, "Okay."

Rita knew what *that* meant!

She played the game and ran very fast—until she slipped and fell down. *Ss-s-zip!* there was a hole in the knee of her new stocking.

Rita got up. She didn't cry. Instead, she used one of her new English words. She looked at the hole in her stocking and said, "Hello." This made everyone smile.

She used one of her other words to say "good-bye" to the boy who was chasing her. Then she ran faster than she thought she could run and touched base. And then she said, "Okay!"

Everyone, even the kids on the other team, laughed and cheered. And Rita smiled the way she used to smile in Puerto Rico. She had a skinned knee and a hole in her stocking, but she smiled because now she felt at home. She had friends. Suddenly this new country felt right—as right as her old one.

This story might be the story of someone in *your* family — of one of your parents, or of *their* parents, or perhaps of their grandparents. Maybe someone in your family started out just as Rita and Juan did. Maybe they came from another country and were lonely at first.

Then one day something happened, just as something happened to Rita. It was not a very big thing, perhaps, but it made somebody feel at home.

Ask your mother or father where your family came from. Ask how they came. On a sailing ship? A steamship? A jet plane?

Why did they come? What happened to make them feel at home in the new place?

Too Short, Too Tall, Too Fat, Too Thin

Bill was shortest in his class
   and wanted to be tall.
"I'd have a lot more friends," he thought,
   "if I were not so small."

      His *friends* said—
"Bill is kind and gentle
   and a really clever guy.
You can tell when he is teasing
   by the twinkle in his eye.
      . . . I like Bill."

Jim was tallest in his class
    and wished that he could shrink.
"My friends expect too much, because
    I'm younger than they think."

        His *friends* said—
"Jim is sort of quiet,
    but he's still a lot of fun.
And if you've lost your pencil,
    he's the boy who'll lend you one.
        . . . I like Jim."

"If I were not so big," said Sid,
  "so very round and fat,
I'd have more fun, and make a run
  each time I came to bat."

       His *friends* said—
  "Sidney's good at talking
    and making long reports.
He cheers our school to victory
  in all the different sports.
        . . . I like Sid."

"Because I'm thin—just bones and skin—"
    said Harold to himself,
"I'm going to exercise with weights!"
    and took them from the shelf.

        His *friends* said—
"If you are having trouble
    with science or with math,
You'd better talk to Harold,
    and you'll get back on the path.
        . . . I like Harold."

How to Catch a Giraffe

How did the giraffes you see in this picture get to the zoo?
They weren't born in the zoo.

They didn't walk or run or swim to get to the zoo.

These giraffes had to travel many miles over mountains and rivers and even cross an ocean before they reached the zoo.

The story of their journey begins on the hot, dusty plains of Africa when these long-legged, long-necked fellows were only one year old.

The men who trap wild animals say this is just the right age for a giraffe to be captured. A one-year-old giraffe is small enough to be shipped to the zoo without getting hurt. And being fed and cared for by strange people doesn't seem to frighten it for very long.

Catching almost any wild animal is difficult and often dangerous. The giraffe is one of the fastest of all animals. Animal trappers can't run nearly so fast as a giraffe. So when they go hunting giraffes for a zoo, the hunters ride in a high-wheeled automobile that can go rolling over the grasslands where there are no roads.

When they get very close, the hunters act like cowboys— maybe we should call them giraffeboys. They stand up in the automobile and whirl a rope and try to drop the lasso loop over the giraffe's head.

Roping the giraffe is only the beginning of the job.

The giraffe is then herded into a high, open crate and taken by truck to an animal camp. It's kept there until the animal trainers and doctors who run the camp decide the giraffe is ready for the trip to the zoo.

Now, a giraffe is no ordinary animal. Its neck and legs are so long that it can't be shipped on an airplane. And so, with one of the trainers, the giraffe rides in a truck, on a train, and finally on a ship. The trainer makes sure that the giraffe eats the right foods and is kept safe and warm on the long journey.

After the ship lands, the giraffe gets one last ride on a truck and train—to the last stop. The zoo!

Except for fat, heavy animals like the rhinoceros, most wild animals are shipped to zoos by airplane. For animals that are used to living in deserts or jungles, the airplanes are heated.

The people who catch wild animals and take them to zoos have to know as much about taking care of animals as a zoo keeper does.

Gold Is Where You Find It

All your life you will be told—
"All that glitters is not gold."

But all gold glitters. *Glitter* means "to shine
brightly." Stars glitter. So do shiny pans.

Gold is hard to find. But some people are
lucky. One man fell off his horse and rolled
down a hillside, kicking up a piece of gold
as big as a chicken egg! He started digging
and found gold all over the hillside.

At the beginning all gold was in the
ground. The rain washed some of it down
the mountain slopes. Men looked for
the glitter of gold in the bottoms of
clear-water creeks. Gold is so
heavy that it stayed in the low
places until found.

Not all gold is under the water
or near the top of the ground.
Some is in rock so far under
the ground that miners have
to dig a deep hole, or *mine
shaft,* to get to it.

In the long-ago days of knights and castles, people tried every way they could think of to *make* gold. They boiled rocks in huge pots. They crushed the rocks into powder. They mixed the powder with such odd things as insect wings and fish scales.

Today we think all this was pretty foolish. But long ago, people thought that by doing such things they might change rocks into gold.

Why do you think they tried so hard to find gold and to make it? What's so wonderful about gold?

Gold glitters and gleams like a million sunbeams playing tag. Most people say that it is the prettiest of all the metals.

There's another good thing about gold. It can be hammered into beautiful shapes—rings and bracelets, cups and plates, beads and statues, coins and crowns.

You could keep gold all your life, and it would hardly change at all. Even in a thousand years it wouldn't change. It doesn't rust like iron. Or turn black or green like copper pennies. It stays bright and shiny.

Gold is also rare, which means there isn't much of it anywhere in the world. When there isn't very much of a thing that is pretty or useful, nearly everybody wants it. That is one reason why gold has been used for money—because everyone wants it.

Long ago, when anybody wanted a new horse or some land or food or clothes or almost anything, all he had to do was trade some gold for it. If he had *enough* gold.

Certainly in those days when gold was used for money almost everywhere, nobody ever seemed to have enough of it. And people who had it were always afraid that someone would steal it. After America was discovered, treasure ships sailed away with gold that had been stolen from the Indians. Then pirates tried to stop the treasure ships and steal the gold for themselves.

Today, divers sometimes go down to the bottom of the ocean to look for the gold that was lost when some of the treasure ships were wrecked.

The Special Long Sleep

What's this ground squirrel doing?

It looks as if it's just asleep for the night, but it's not. It's not pretending, either. It's *hibernating*.

Hibernating is a special lo-o-o-ng sleep. This ground squirrel has gone to sleep for the whole winter.

How can it do this? Doesn't it need to eat?

No.

Why doesn't it?

When they're running around, animals *do* need food—just as cars need gasoline. Without gasoline, a car stops. Without food, an animal can live for only a short time. Then it will die.

In the summer there's usually plenty of food for animals to eat.

In the winter there's less food to be found. Some animals go south, where it's warmer, and find food there. Some bury nuts and seeds under the ground in the summertime, and in the winter they can dig them up.

Other animals do as the ground squirrel does. They go to sleep for most of the winter—they hibernate.

Woodchucks, hamsters, bats, and hedgehogs are some of the other animals that can hibernate. Some birds, fish, insects, and butterflies hibernate, too.

When an animal takes its special long sleep, its heart almost stops beating. Its blood almost stops flowing. It gets very, very cold, almost—but not quite—cold enough to freeze. And it almost stops breathing. Some hibernating animals take only one breath every few minutes.

When the weather gets warm again, the heart of the hibernating animal begins to beat faster. The blood runs faster. The animal breathes faster, too. Its body becomes warm. It gets up and goes to join the other animals looking for food. It is spring!

In fairy tales and legends, such as "Sleeping Beauty" and "Rip Van Winkle," we read about people who sleep for a very long time. Rip Van Winkle slept for 20 years, and when he woke up, he found that everything had changed. He had become an old man with a white beard.

In real life, people can't hibernate. They get hungry and wake up ready for breakfast.

But some scientists think that maybe sometime we *can* find a way to hibernate. Then we could get in a spaceship and "go to sleep" and wake up a long time later on a star.

HICCUPS

I think there's nothing—*hic!*—so bad
  As—*hic!*—cups that you cannot stop.
They start so suddenly. They—*hic!*—
  They make your—*hic!*—words jump and hop.

Sometimes they're quick like *hic! hic! hic!*
  Sometimes they're slow—you think they're through.
Then, when you don't expect—*hic!*—them,
  Another—*hic!*—comes out of you.

Your aunt will tell you, "Hold your breath
  And count to ten—but very slow.
Now are they gone?" You're not quite sure;
  You'll have to wait and see—*hic!*—No.

Your Uncle Pete says, "Bow your head
  And drink some water upside down."
But that gets water in your nose
  And—*hic!*—it makes you sneeze and frown.

Your friends all tell you things to do;
  Each one of them has got a trick.
You try them all but nothing works;
  You keep—*hic!*—cupping—*hic! hic! hic!*

You—*hic!*— for hours—and as you do,
  Your body shakes from toe to top.
And then as quickly as they came,
  With one last—*hic!*—your hiccups stop.

The Lost Necklace

Many years ago a young girl sat as still as she could while a man carved her picture into a large stone in the palace wall.

She was glad that he was almost finished, because it had taken many days, and she wanted to run and play with her brother. Her fingers tugged at the golden hawk that hung on a string of red beads around her neck. She tugged until the necklace broke

and the beads scattered on the ground.

The carver picked them all up and promised to fix them so they would never break again.

"Oh, I hope you can," the girl said. "They were a birthday present from my father."

After the necklace had been put together again, the man looked for the girl. She was not playing outside the walls with the other children, but her brother was.

"Will you give this necklace to your sister?" the man asked.

The boy took the necklace, but when he saw his sister coming, he

hid it behind a small statue. Then he told his sister what he had done.

"Don't tell me where!" she cried. "Let me find it myself."

After that, "finding the necklace" became one of their favorite games.

When the girl grew up, she gave the necklace to her daughter, who in turn gave it to *her* daughter.

Then, one day, there was a terrible war. The people of the city ran away, leaving many things behind. One of the things left was the pretty necklace.

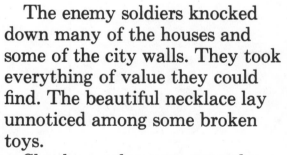

The enemy soldiers knocked
down many of the houses and
some of the city walls. They took
everything of value they could
find. The beautiful necklace lay
unnoticed among some broken
toys.

Slowly, as the years went by,
the drifting sands covered the
city and the walls. Now the
necklace was hidden again.

Each year, the city was buried
deeper and deeper. Camel caravans passed over it, and nobody
even knew there was a city
buried under the desert.

Then, one day, some men came looking for buried cities. A freshwater spring and the way the sand had been heaped by the wind told them something might be buried there. The men didn't know about the city or the pretty necklace, but they started digging.

They dug carefully and slowly. They dug for days and days . . . deeper and deeper . . . wider and wider. Still they found nothing.

But one day . . .

A worker shouted from his digging, "I've found something! A wall!"

Now they dug even more carefully, sometimes gently brushing the soil from the wall with their fingers. When the palace wall was uncovered, they brushed the earth from the young girl's picture. They read her name and wondered who she was.

A few days later, as they dug out one of the royal bedrooms, a tiny red bump appeared in the sand. Carefully, they brushed the earth away until a string of dark-red beads with a tiny golden hawk was uncovered.

One of the men recognized the beads.

"They're the beads the girl on the wall is wearing!" he said. "She must have been a princess."

Now this treasure from the past is in a museum. People from all over the world come to look at it and try to imagine the young princess who wore it.

Here and there throughout the world, other men and women are digging—looking for cities that have been buried for so long that they have been forgotten. Each time one is discovered, a little more is learned about people who lived long, long ago.

Little Big Man

Today was a very special day for Little Tree Leaf, the Indian boy. It was a day of many tests. If he passed, he would no longer be thought of as a boy in his tribe. He would be a man—a hunter among hunters, a warrior among warriors.

In the arrow-shooting test, Little Tree Leaf put more arrows into the mossy tree stump than anyone else except Rain Cloud. And he stayed longer than anyone on the back of a wildly kicking and running horse.

But on the other tests, Little Tree Leaf did not do very well. He was not so tall or so strong as the other boys of the tribe. In the wrestling test, Boy-Who-Eats-Much threw him to the ground and sat on him, holding him down while everybody laughed.

In the pretend fight, which was almost a real fight—with real spears and stone battle-axes—Little Tree Leaf was knocked down, cut and bleeding, beaten by Wolf Cub. In the running test, three other boys ran farther, and many ran faster.

Six boys passed the day's tests, and Little Tree Leaf was not one of them. Then, to his surprise, the chief gave him a long look.

"The boy tries hard," the chief said. "He never stops trying. He has earned his chance to take the last test. Let him go with the six winners to find a cave in the hills."

The test of the cold cave was given every year to boys who hoped to become braves. With no blanket to protect him from the cold, each boy had to go into the hills and find a cave and then live in it *alone* for four days and four nights. During all this time, he was forbidden to eat food or even to drink water.

The bigger boys found caves first. Little Tree Leaf had to climb nearly to the top of a mountain before he found one. He stood outside and stared into the cave's dark mouth. Glowing in the dark, two fiery eyes looked out at him!

Something was already in there. What was it?

Was it a porcupine in the cave? A fox? It might even be a

wildcat or a wolf. Whatever it was, Little Tree Leaf knew that to pass the test and become a warrior, he must be brave enough to make the animal leave the cave.

Stooping, he picked up the biggest rock he could lift and hurled it inside. The echoes of the rolling rock sounded from the cave — and with the echoes, a low and angry *gr-r-r-r--ow-l-l!*

Little Tree Leaf wanted to run. But he didn't run. Instead, he talked back to the animal. Patting his hand against his open mouth, he answered the growl with a loud, fierce war whoop, *"Yi-yi-yi-yi-ee-ow-w-w!"*

Then the Indian boy waited with his bow and arrow.

The animal that padded angrily from the cave, snarling and showing white teeth in a red mouth, was more dangerous than any that Little Tree Leaf had expected. The animal that glared at him was a mountain lion—perhaps the very one that last week at the water hole had sprung upon a girl, Star Blanket, clawing and biting her before it was driven away.

Neither Little Tree Leaf nor any of his comrades had ever fought a mountain lion. He didn't want to fight one now. But the great cat gave him no choice. It sprang at him with jaws open and claws outstretched.

The bowstring made a sharp twang as Little Tree Leaf shot his arrow. His aim was good. The arrow struck the mountain lion, and the beast fell to the ground so close to Little Tree Leaf that its claws raked the dust between his feet.

Little Tree Leaf stepped over the dead mountain lion and went into the dark cave. He was cold and hungry and thirsty. And he was afraid that the lion's mate might return. But to prove that he was brave enough to be a warrior, he stayed in the cave for four days and four nights, ready for anything that might happen.

Afterward, he carried the tail of the dead mountain lion back to the village and gave it to the chief.

The chief raised the boy's arm high. "You have passed the test," he said. "You can hang the lion's tail at the door of your lodge as your first hunting trophy."

In a dance and feast that lasted all night, Little Tree Leaf was made a warrior of the tribe. Now he could hunt with the chief and the other warriors. He could answer the war drums and fight beside his Indian brothers.

And he was given a new name, a man's name—Little-Man-Who-Hunts-Mountain Lions.

What Kind of Bug Is This?

If you answer, "A ladybug," you are right about its nickname. (It is also known as a ladybird beetle.) And you may know a little verse about it—

Ladybug, ladybug,
Fly away home. . . .

But the ladybug isn't a true bug. Not every creeping, crawling, wriggling, flying creature is a bug, as many people think. Bugs are only part of a big group of little creatures called *insects*. For example, a ladybug doesn't have thickened front wings folded over its back the way true bugs have. And it doesn't have the long, beaky mouthparts for sucking the juices of plants.

There are many different kinds of insects. They may be as tiny as a dot or as big as a mouse. They may be long or short, fat or slim, black or brightly colored. Some insects fly, some crawl, some hop.

But in some ways all full-grown insects are alike. The easiest way to know an insect is to count its legs. All insects have six legs —three pairs.

Some of these are insects.

Insects have bodies with three parts—
a head with a pair of feelers, or *antennas;*
a middle part, called *thorax,* with legs and usually wings growing from it;
a hind part, called *abdomen.*

All insects, like the dragonfly above, have a shell-like covering that they shed from time to time as they grow.

Insects have many different habits.

Bee

Makes honey

Butterfly

Flies south
in late summer

Cricket

First summer
concert singer

Fly

Walks upside down
on the ceiling

Doodlebug

Walks backward in circles

Water Strider

Skates on the water

Mosquito

The ladies sing and sting

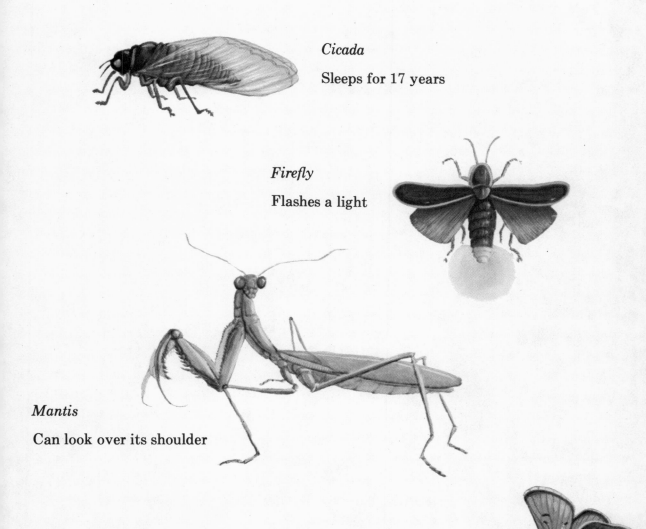

Cicada

Sleeps for 17 years

Firefly

Flashes a light

Mantis

Can look over its shoulder

A caterpillar is an insect, too. It doesn't look like an insect, but it will after it turns into a butterfly. Now when you look at this picture, you know why the ant, the butterfly, the bee, and the caterpillar are insects. The earthworm isn't an insect. It doesn't have *any* legs. And the centipede has *too many* legs! Why isn't the spider an insect?

From Page to Knight

Hilary threw himself on his bed of straw. He was tired. He had never, *ever* been so tired.

His legs hurt from running, his arms ached from carrying, and his head still buzzed from trying to remember all the orders he'd been given—"Hilary, run to the stable——" "Hilary, fetch my cloak——" "Hilary, carry this box to the Great Hall——"

Hilary was seven years old, and his first day at Lord Sutton's castle had ended at last.

Hilary hoped to become a knight when he grew up, and today his years of training had begun. For a while he would serve in the castle as a page, dashing about on errands for all the lords and ladies. And each day he would also learn some of the many things a knight must know.

That very afternoon he'd been thumped, bumped, and bruised during his first lesson in the art of horsemanship. He had been taught how to fall from his horse without breaking his bones or spraining his ankles.

"But my bones feel as if they were broken," he thought. "Will it always be so hard? Will I always be so tired?"

That night Hilary fell asleep in the room where all the pages lived. Before the sun rose, they would all have to get up again so that they could take breakfast to the ladies of the castle.

Lady Sutton gave Hilary lessons in politeness—"Hilary, you must not talk with food in your mouth." "Did you remember to leave the largest pieces of meat for others?" "How untidy you are!" "Remember to keep yourself washed and combed." Hilary was learning not to argue but to do what he was told as fast as he could. The pages often grumbled to one another, "How can we ever remember all these rules?"

Hilary learned to stand behind Lord Sutton's place at the table, serving his lordship's food and pouring water for washing the hands at mealtime. In those days people used their fingers, not forks or spoons, to pick up their food.

As Hilary grew older, he learned to ride so well that he could make a horse turn, stop, or rear on its hind legs at the softest command.

The pages had a favorite game. Astride their horses, they would charge a metal target and try to strike it with a long wooden pole. If the rider missed the target's center, the target would twirl and topple the rider from his horse. Hilary and the other pages roared with laughter when somebody else fell but forgot to laugh when *they* were thrown to the ground.

Hilary spent many happy hours listening to the songs and stories of the wandering minstrels who visited the castle. When he had learned some of the words and tunes, he began to play a stringed instrument called a *lute*. He loved to sing about brave men and brave deeds.

Lord Sutton and his men often talked to the pages about fairness and kindness—"You must be fair to others in games, and even in battle you must always fight according to the rules. A knight is always truthful and always kind and always polite to women and children."

To prepare himself for the hardships of battle, Hilary learned to go without food for as long as two whole days and without sleep for a whole night. Often he was covered with cuts and bruises from practicing with swords and lances and with the long poles called *quarterstaffs*.

For seven years Hilary worked as a page. Then Lord Sutton chose Hilary to serve as his companion, or *squire*, on the battlefield. If Lord Sutton dropped or broke his sword, Hilary was to hand him another. If Lord Sutton was ever toppled from his horse, Hilary would have to rush to his side and help him up.

One of Hilary's duties was polishing his lord's helmet, shield, and other armor until they shone. Sometimes he would try on the helmet, and using the shield as a mirror, he'd look into it and whisper the name he would be given as knight—Sir Hilary. But most of the time Hilary practiced with his sword and lance, preparing himself for the day he would ride into battle as a knight.

One day Lord Sutton and his knights and squires were returning from a neighboring castle. Suddenly, deep in the forest, they were attacked by a bloodthirsty band of robbers who hoped to steal their valuable armor and weapons. *Clang . . . clash!* Swords and lances struck against armor. Knights and robbers fell wounded from their horses. Men shouted. The horses neighed and reared.

Hilary was fighting for his life when, out of the corner of his eye, he saw that Lord Sutton was in desperate danger. He raised his lance just in time to stop a bandit's sword from killing Lord Sutton.

When the bandits were finally driven away, Hilary's master said to him, "You saved my life, giving no thought to your own danger. Your brave deed will be rewarded."

Soon afterward, before the lord and the lady of the castle and all the knights and squires and pages, Hilary was made a knight. His mother and father were there, smiling proudly. First came the ladies, one by one, to buckle on Hilary's new armor. Lord Sutton gave him a great heavy sword and golden spurs, which were a sign to everyone that Hilary was a knight.

Then Hilary knelt. Lord Sutton touched him on the shoulder with a sword, saying, "I dub thee knight! Be gallant, be courteous, be loyal. Arise, Sir Hilary."

Hilary silently promised that he would be all these things. Then, as he looked up, he saw his reflection in Lord Sutton's shield. He saw his own shining armor and proud face. *Sir* Hilary, at last!

The Bear That Isn't a Bear

This roly-poly little animal has shiny black eyes that look like wet licorice candy. Its nose is shiny black, too, and pressed against its face between its bushy gray ears. If you found it under a Christmas tree, you might think it was a toy teddy bear.

But "roly-poly" is a real animal. It lives only in Australia. It is called a *koala*, and it looks so much like a toy bear that you want to turn it around just to see if it has a key in its back so that you can wind it up.

But koalas aren't bears. They belong to the same family as kangaroos. Animals of this family are called *pouch* animals. That's because the mother carries her baby around in a pouch in the front of her stomach. It's like a built-in papoose basket, only it's in the front instead of the back.

When they are first born, koala babies are smaller even than a little finger. Only one koala baby is born at a time. After about six months the koala baby is ready to explore the world. But not on its own feet. It comes out of the pouch and climbs up on its

mother's back. For six months it rides on her back everywhere she goes until it's almost as big as she is.

It sounds as if its mother spoils it. But she can be strict when it doesn't behave. If it's too naughty, she'll even put it over her knee and spank it!

The koala drinks dew and eats nothing but leaves from eucalyptus and blue gum trees.

Koalas love people and make wonderful pets. When a koala likes you, it puts its arms around your neck and hugs you!

Look at the Leaves

In some parts of the world it gets very cold in the winter and very warm in the summer. In these places you can tell what time of the year it is just by noticing two things: the kinds of things that children are doing and what's happening to the leaves on the broad-leaved trees.

Spring leaves—
March, April, May
leaves are light, bright
green. They look very, very
clean—as if each one had been
carefully washed and hung out to dry
in the sun. Some trees have blossoms
among their fresh green leaves. It's
time to fly kites in the fresh breezes
blowing up the hill. It's time to play
outdoors. Good-bye, walls and winter chills!

Summer leaves—
June, July, August
leaves are green, too; but
instead of being a light, sunny
green, they are dark and shaded. They
look as if they'd been colored by someone who
pressed down very hard on his crayon. There are
no blossoms among these leaves. They are so thick and
heavy that you wonder how the branches can hold them all. Now
it's time for bicycling, for swimming, or singing around a campfire.

Autumn leaves—
September, October,
November leaves are red
and yellow and gold. They
come drifting down from tree branches
like little airplanes floating. These bright,
fire-colored leaves warn us that we'd better light
the firē again. Cold weather is coming! It's time to
walk through the brown grass and fallen leaves—after school.

Winter leaves—
December, January, February
leaves are dull gray or dusty brown.
Most of them lie on the ground near the
tree on which they grew. They look tired and
sad. But wait! Look up at the branches of the tree!
Do you see all those little bumps? They are the buds.
From the buds tiny leaves and blossoms will grow for next year.
But now it's time to build a snowman, go Christmas shopping,
sit by the fire. And almost before you know it, the light,
bright green leaves will tell you that it's spring again!

Who's in the Library?

The books in your library were written by many different men and women from all over the world. Some lived long, long ago. Some are still alive today. Even those who are not alive can still tell you things—*in their books*.

If all of these writers could suddenly be in your library, they would fill all the rooms, hang out the windows, and cover the roof! They would fill the street and spread through the neighborhood!

Isn't it lucky that libraries are filled with books instead of writers? The writers couldn't be in all libraries at once.

But their books can.

In nearly every large town and city, people can go to libraries to read the wise and beautiful and exciting and funny things that have been written.

The Duck's Dinosaur

A library is a house for books.

Pam stands and looks . . . and looks . . . and *looks!*

Books on the shelves and on the table. Books on the chairs and on the stairs. More books, it seems, than she could ever read.

With so many books everywhere, how can Pam ever find the one special book she wants?

If you know the ABC's, and if you know how to count, you can find any book in the library all by yourself. But if you want her to, the library lady will help you. She's called a *librarian*.

Pam: I want to read a book, please, called *The Dinosaur's Duck*.

First, the librarian takes Pam to the *card catalog*. This is a piece of furniture that looks more like a shiny box than anything else. In the box are many small drawers filled with white cards.

Each card has the name of a book on it. There is a card for every book in the library.

Librarian: I'm sorry. There is no card here for *The Dinosaur's Duck*. Are you sure that is the right name of the book?

Pam: Maybe it was *The Duck's Dinosaur*.

Librarian (smiling, as she finds the card): Oh yes, here it is— *The Duck's Dinosaur*. Now we'll go look for it, Pam.

Pam: So many, many books! How can we ever find the special one I want?

Librarian: It's easy, Pam. You'll see. The card with the name of your book on it also has the name of the author and a special letter on it. The book you want shows the name of the author and the same letter. . . . Here are the E's—we're getting close, Pam. Your book is on one of these shelves right here.

Librarian: Here's your book, Pam—*The Duck's Dinosaur*.

Pam (delightedly): Why, it's just like finding somebody's house when you know the name of the street!

Back to the desk they go with the book.

To help her remember who borrowed *The Duck's Dinosaur*, the librarian writes Pam's name down.

She stamps a date on the book card to show how many days Pam can keep the book at home.

Pam: As soon as I read this book, I'll be back for another one.

How would you like to be the library lady? Or the library man? You can—at home—with your own books.

The Workers That Don't Get Tired

Which one is a machine?

They all are. A machine is something that people use to help them do work.

There are many machines in your home, and almost everything that isn't a machine was *made* by a machine.

A machine called the *alarm clock* probably awakens your family each morning.

The electric shaver and the toothbrush are machines. So are the broom and the spoon.

A machine makes the electricity that makes the heat that toasts the toast, cooks the eggs, perks the coffee, lights the room, and sometimes heats the house.

A machine pumps the water that you use every day in so many ways. The machine pumps it through the pipes, and your hand on a machine called a *faucet* turns the water on and off.

And when you leave the place where you live, if you have very far to go, you'll probably go there *in* a machine

or *on* a machine.

It would take a long time to name all the things we use that are made with machines.

It's quicker to name a few that *aren't* made with machines. A sand castle that we make with our hands might be one thing. Or a pot made with clay found in the ground and then baked in the sun. Or a paper airplane that we make by folding.

Can you think of anything else that *isn't* made with the help of a machine?

Sometimes many simple machines are put together to make one *complicated* machine. *Complicated* is a big word for something with many parts.

An alarm clock has many parts—sometimes more than a hundred. Among these parts are a spring, wheels, a bell, a bell hammer, and hands. Each of these parts is a simple machine with a special job to do. All of these simple machines working together make one complicated machine called the *alarm clock*.

The spring turns the big wheel. The big wheel turns three other wheels. One of these wheels turns the hour hand, slowly. Another turns the minute hand, faster. There is another spring that turns a wheel that makes the bell hammer go back and forth, hitting the bell.

Each part in the clock makes the next part move. This works something like a train, the engine of which pulls the next car, which pulls the next car, which pulls the next car, which pulls the caboose.

There was once a man who thought it was fun to think up work for silly machines to do. His drawings of these funny machines made people laugh.

Today people use the man's name when they talk about such silly machines. They call them Rube Goldbergs.

Here is a silly machine you could use to wake up your dog.

You pull the string to lift the cover and let the fly out. The Champ Fly Swatter swats at the fly. The other end of the board rolls the ball down the chute to knock the pepper over, to make the man sneeze, to bop the painter, to make him fall back, to drop the ax, to cut the rope, to drop the cat, to wake the dog.

Can you think of an easier way to wake the dog?

How We Move

Inside our skin there are bones. Our fingers can feel them almost everywhere. One bone is attached to another, and when the bones move, we move.

But our bones cannot move themselves.

Our *muscles* move them.

Our bones are covered with muscles. The muscles move them in many directions. That is the job of muscles—to move things.

How do our muscles move our bones?

Our muscles move our bones by pulling them. Muscles always pull—they never push.

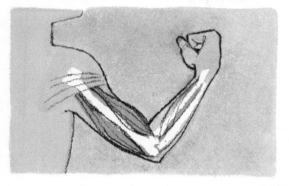

The pink muscle is doing the pulling to bend the arm.

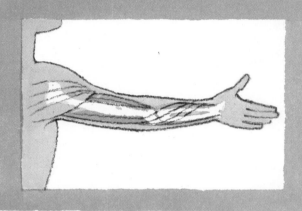

Now a different muscle is pulling to straighten the arm.

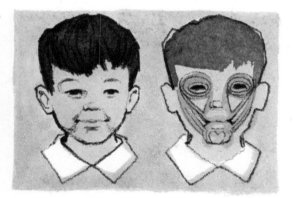

We can feel the jaw muscles in our cheeks become hard as they pull our jaw closed when we bite.

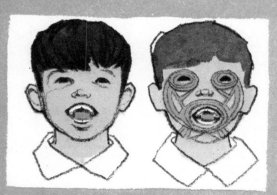

We can feel the muscle under our jaw pull to open our mouth wide.

Some muscles don't move *bones*. They move *other* things.

Our heart is the muscle that pumps the blood. To understand how it works, imagine a few children standing in a circle with their arms hooked together. If they all *pull* at the same time, what happens?

They squeeze the circle smaller.

When the heart squeezes like this, the blood is pumped out and through the body.

Tiny muscles move our eyes up, down, and from side to side.

The muscles of our mouth, lips, and face move to make us smile or frown.

Without muscles the skin would be like a bag. And a man would be a bag of bones!

Why the Oceans Are Salty

If you ever get a mouthful of ocean water, you'll find it's very salty.

How did it get this way?

Rivers are the oceans' saltshakers. Almost every river in the world finally pours its waters into an ocean. While the river is running to the sea, it loosens some of the land and carries it along. The land is made up of rocks and soil, which contain minerals. One of these minerals is salt.

You can't taste the salt in river water because the river doesn't carry much salt at any one time. And you can't taste it in most lakes because as one river brings a little salt in, another river carries it out. It has taken rivers millions and millions of years to pour enough salt into the oceans to make ocean water taste salty.

Salt water is not good for people to drink. It is not good for plants. We can't stop the rivers from carrying salt from the land to the sea, but we *can* do something so that we can use the waters of the sea for people and plants.

Scientists are working on machines that will take salt out of ocean water. Some of these machines work very well, but they cost too much to use as much as we would like. So the scientists keep trying to find cheaper ways to do the job.

When you grow up, you may be one of the people who invent a new way to take salt out of ocean water. That would be better than discovering a shipwrecked pirate's treasure. The people and plants on the lands of this Earth need nonsalty ocean water more than gold or jewels!

Diving and Swimming Champ

Floating lazily on its back—rocking in the icy ocean waves—this otter might seem just to be taking a nap.

Not true! If you look closely, you'll see this furry fellow is hard at work getting the tasty meat out of a clamshell.

A strange way to eat, lying on your back! But that's how sea otters often do it. They use their front paws as hands, and their stomachs for tables!

Most amazing of all, the sea otter sometimes uses a stone to help it get food. It is one of the few animals smart enough to use a tool. This diving sea otter didn't go to the ocean bottom only to gather clams. While it was down there, it picked up a stone to use in cracking open the clamshells!

An otter's big webbed feet are just right for swimming and diving deep under the water. Otters are among the fastest-swimming animals.

When night comes, this clever fisherman likes to wrap itself in some giant seaweed near shore. The weeds make a soft nest for sleeping and also help keep the otter safe from dangerous sharks.

If you should see a whiskery, shiny animal with a long, skinny body sliding down a muddy bank into a river—*splash*—it would look like a sea otter. But it isn't.

It's a river otter. Playful and funny, it makes a delightful pet.

River otters are champion swimmers, too. The river otter knows just how to build a nest lined with leaves and grass—not in water but under the ground—in a tunnel that it digs near a river or a lake.

Sometimes the nest will be buried under the roots of a tree. But no matter where the nest is, it's warm and safe for the whole family.

Baby otters don't know how to swim when they're born. The babies that are afraid of the water are carried on their mother's back until they're ready to take off on their own. Then they dive for good things to eat — fish, frogs, snails, and shellfish.

Not Invited

What Sue said—

She didn't ask *me* to her party!
I wish I could figure out why.
You know whom she did invite? Marty!
(And Marty threw sand in her eye!)

Mom says, "I'm sure Mary meant to.
I'm sure that she only forgot."
But how can your best friend forget you?
Excuses! It still hurts a lot.

Mary must surely remember
The times when we had so much fun.
When she moved to our block in September,
She said I was Friend Number One.

You know what? I'm getting a notion!
Yes, I'll give a big party, too!
With gallons of punch—oh, an ocean!
And millions of fun things to do.

My cake will collapse the whole table—
Too big to get inside the door.
We'll eat until no one is able
To swallow a single bite more.

We'll have oodles of cookies and candy,
Each one will get ten pounds or so.
I'll ask Marcia and Linda and Sandy,
Not Mary! *Not* Mary. OH, NO!

What Mary said—

Just everyone's here at my party,
Except for my special friend, Sue.
There's even that terrible Marty,
(And you know what *he* used to do).

I'm sure that Sue thinks I forgot her.
I didn't! I didn't at all!
The letter I carefully wrote her
Fell back of a chair in the hall.

Sue never got asked to my party.
Her lost invitation was found

When Marty, that terrible Marty,
Started pushing the chairs all around.

Then Daddy said, "I'll go and get her."
I'm waiting. The others are, too. . . .
They're here! And there's Sue with my letter!
There's Sue! *There's Sue!* THERE'S SUE!

Oh, now it's a wonderful party,
With ever so much we can do.
Who saved it? That terrible Marty!
(Now *he's* my best friend next to Sue.)

Choosing a Pet

William stood in front of the cage, watching the monkey swinging upside down.

Mr. Gage, the owner of the pet shop, smiled at William. "Just looking?" he asked.

"No," William said. "My Aunt Vera gave me $3.00 for my birthday. And I worked and saved $4.15. That makes $7.15. My mother said I can buy a pet."

"But not a monkey," he whispered so that the monkey wouldn't hear. "Mom says monkeys are too messy."

"Besides, they need a lot of room," said Mr. Gage. "That's why this one's in such a big cage."

Rules for keeping all pets
1. Know what to feed your pet, how much and how often.
2. Always have fresh water where your pet can get it.
3. Keep your pet's home clean.
4. Never frighten your pet. If you do, it may scratch or bite you.

Rules for keeping fish
1. Feed fish once each day. Too much food will make them sick.
2. Don't put too many fish in the same tank. Every inch of fish needs a gallon of water.
3. Fish need light but shouldn't be left all day in sunlight.
4. Don't frighten the fish with a sharp noise or flashing light.
5. If your fish keep coming to the top when it isn't feeding time, they may need more air in the water. Your pet shop has a special pump to put more air in the water.

William turned to the goldfish.
"What kind of fish are those?"

"Those are goldfish," answered Mr. Gage.

"I wonder if goldfish have any gold in them," said William.

"I don't think so," said Mr. Gage. "They're just gold colored."

"Oh," said William. "What can they do?"

"Do? They swim and eat fish food and . . . swim."

"I want something that'll crawl over my hand."

Mr. Gage thought for a moment. "How about a nice turtle? A turtle can swim and crawl over your hand."

He put a small turtle on William's hand. Suddenly the turtle's head and legs disappeared.

> *Rules for keeping turtles*
> 1. Turtles need an inch or two of water to swim in.
> 2. They also need a flat rock to crawl onto when they want to dry or sun themselves.
> 3. If a turtle has a painted design on its shell, remove the design by scraping gently. The design may also be removed with a little nail polish remover.

"Why does it pull its head in?" asked William. "And its legs?"

"To protect itself," Mr. Gage answered.

While Mr. Gage went to get a cardboard box for the turtle, William looked at the small cages with wheels in them.

"And I want one of these," he said, pointing to the cage, "so that my turtle can walk on the wheel and play."

"Turtles don't walk on wheels," said Mr. Gage. "They like to play in a tank that has rocks in it and a little water."

"I want something that'll swim and crawl on my hand and walk on the wheel," said William.

Mr. Gage couldn't think of what animal that would be.

"A mouse can *run* on the wheel *and* crawl on your hand," he said. "It's a clean pet and doesn't take much space. But it doesn't like to swim."

Mr. Gage put a white mouse into the cage. The mouse jumped onto the wheel and started to run.

"How do you like the mouse?" Mr. Gage asked.

"Fine!" answered William.

"Good," said Mr. Gage.

"But my mother doesn't like mice," said William sadly.

William looked at the hamsters and a guinea pig. They were not mice, and the hamsters liked to run on the wheel.

The guinea pig had a beautiful black-and-white coat.

"What does it eat?" asked William.

"Grain and greens like lettuce, cabbage, and grass. In the winter it needs a few drops of cod-liver oil every week."

This made William smile.

"Stroke its back," said Mr. Gage. "The oil from your hand is good for its fur."

"Its ears are very small," said William, finally.

Mr. Gage set a large rabbit in front of William.

> *Rules for keeping rabbits*
> 1. They don't eat meat.
> 2. They shouldn't eat lettuce. They can eat grass, carrots, bran, hay, clover, oats, and a little cabbage. They like pellets best.
> 3. Rabbits need to gnaw. A thick twig is fine for this.

"Gosh!" said William, "look at *those* ears."

"And it can hop," said Mr. Gage, "and eat out of your hand."

"Can it sing?" asked William. "Bob's canary can whistle and sing."

"I never heard of a singing rabbit," Mr. Gage answered.

William listened to the canaries sing but decided he wanted a pet he could play with.

The greenish blue parakeet sat on his finger.

"Parakeets can do tricks," said Mr. Gage. "And play with their own special toys."

"Can it talk?" William asked.

"Not yet," answered Mr. Gage, "but you can teach it."

"Not much!" said a strange voice behind them. The red-and-yellow parrot looked at them over its funny hooked beak.

"Who said that?" William asked.

"The parrot did," answered Mr. Gage. "You can teach parrots to say a few words, too."

"How do you do that?" asked William.

"You keep saying something over and over again. After a while the bird learns to say it. But parrots are very expensive, and they need lots of room."

Rules for keeping birds
1. They need a cage large enough to exercise freely.
2. Don't keep them in a hot room, or they will lose their feathers.
3. Have two or more hardwood perches in the cage. The perches should be different sizes so that the bird can rest its feet.
4. Scrape the perch when it gets dirty. Never wash it because the dampness may make your bird sick.

William looked around the pet shop. There were so many pets to choose from. Then he looked up at Mr. Gage. "Well," William asked, shrugging, "what should I get?"

Mr. Gage smiled. "How about a kitten?" he asked. "It has soft fur."

William looked at the kittens in the window pen.

"What can a kitten do?" he asked.

"Well, it's playful. And it'll chase a rolling ball or a piece of string if you pull it. It can't sing, but it certainly can meow and purr."

William stroked the kitten's soft fur. "It feels nice. Will it go with me on walks and do what I tell it?"

"Probably not," answered Mr. Gage. "Cats are not very good at obeying. How about a dog?"

The puppies jumped and yipped in a large pen. When William reached into the pen, one pup caught William's sleeve between its teeth. The pup shook its head back and forth, making William laugh.

"Look!" he said. "This puppy wants to be my pet."

"A dog makes a good pet," said Mr. Gage. "This one is only $5.00, and here's a nice leash for $1.50."

As the dog led William out of the door, William looked at Mr. Gage and laughed. "I didn't choose a pet at all, did I? My pet chose me."

Wagons West

Before there were automobiles or railroad trains in the United States, people traveled west in big covered wagons.

Some traveled to find free land and to make new homes. The country was wild all the way—miles and miles of waving grass, hot deserts, and high mountains. Nobody lived there except Indians. There were no houses, and no stores where people could buy things. No roads anywhere. No bridges over rivers. Buffalo and mountain lions and rattlesnakes and prairie dogs were some of the animals living there.

Let's go with Tad and Ellen and their family as they traveled west across the country on a covered-wagon trip that took many months.

The wagon was painted blue. Its high wheels were red. White sailcloth spread like a balloon to form the roof and the sides.

"Red, white, and blue," Ellen said. "Riding in this wagon will be like the Fourth of July every day!"

"Especially if Indians come whooping at us," Tad said, "and our guns start popping like firecrackers."

"Don't talk about the Indians," his sister said. "I'm scared even before we start."

"We won't be alone," her father comforted her. "We'll travel with other wagons—a whole train of wagons. Now let's start packing this one."

There wasn't room for everything in the wagon. What should
they take?

They had to stay warm, so
they took feather mattresses and
blankets and extra clothes.

They had to eat, so they took

A BARREL OF FLOUR,
FOR MAKING BREAD
ON THE WAY —
A BIG BAG OF BEANS,
A JUG OF SYRUP AND
SOME FAT MEAT THAT
HAD BEEN SALTED AND
SMOKED TO KEEP IT
FROM SPOILING.

They took guns and tools and
kitchen pans. They took seeds
for planting in fields and gardens.
Their milk cow, Bess, would go
with them, and their bulldog,
Sam—although *they* could walk,
of course.

After the wagon was loaded with the things that *had* to go, everybody brought out the things he *hoped* could go. Ellen put two dolls in the wagon, but her father didn't think there would be room for her dollhouse. Tad took a bag of marbles, a spinning top, and a wooden hoop, but he had to leave his toy wagon behind. They took the baby's cradle and Grandmother's old rocking chair.

Six horses pulled the heavy wagon as it rolled out of the yard, jolting and swaying on its long way west. After the family found land in the West, their horses would work on the farm.

Before the wagon got very far west, it was joined by other wagons going the same way.

"When people travel together," the children's father said, "they can help each other if Indians attack or if a wagon breaks down or if anyone runs out of food."

The great wagons rolled slowly in a long line, or train. Scouts rode far ahead to look for drinking water, to find night camping places, to hunt for fresh meat — and to watch for Indians.

Every night the wagons drew up in a tight circle. People and animals stayed inside the circle to be safe from Indians.

After supper a man played a violin—wagon people called it a *fiddle*—while children and grownups danced and sang and clapped their hands and tried not to think of the Indians who were watching from the dark hills.

"Why don't the Indians like us?" Ellen asked her father.

"Because our people are killing the buffalo and taking their land," her father answered. "They want to stop us in any way they can."

Ellen's mother said, "You children stay very, very close to the wagons. It's not safe to wander."

One evening when the wagon train made camp, the word went quickly around that Tad and Ellen were lost. Lost in Indian country!

Men ran to get their rifles. But before a search party had time to leave the camp, the children came running back.

"Look!" they shouted. "Look!"

Ellen clutched a headband made of colored porcupine quills.

Tad held out a bow and arrow. "We met an Indian family!"

"And we traded," Ellen said. "My silver bracelet and Tad's pocketknife and spinning top."

The children's father and mother were shaking their heads as though they couldn't believe that their children had met Indians and come away safely.

Day after day and mile after mile, the great, strong wagons creaked and jolted on their long way west. Finally, the summer was gone, and winter was almost here.

They were in the mountains now—the big, high mountains— with the tired horses pulling the wagons higher and higher—and slower and slower. It seemed to Tad and Ellen that they would *never* reach the top.

But one day they *did*. Stopping for a rest, they looked down and down on the sunny, green world on the other side. Somewhere down there new farms were waiting to be planted. Tall trees were waiting to be cut and made into log houses—and schools. A whole new life was waiting there for the people who had been brave enough to cross the West in a wagon train.

It's Not a Dog at All

Yip–yip–yip!
It *sounds* like a dog.
It even looks a little like a dog.
But even though it is called a *prairie dog*, this cunning little animal, with its thick body and its round head, is not really a dog.

Prairie dogs are called prairie dogs for two reasons. They live in the wide grasslands, or prairies, of the American West; and when they're excited, they make those little *yip–yip–yipping* sounds.

They are really more like squirrels than dogs. But they don't climb trees as squirrels do. Instead, they dig deep tunnels in the ground.

Prairie dogs are friendly little creatures. They live together in "towns" of their very own. There used to be many more prairie dogs than there are now, and they lived in *very* big towns. In some of the prairie-dog towns, there were more prairie dogs than there are people today in some of the biggest cities in the world.

Prairie dogs romp and play in the sun. Or they stir about, hunting wild grasses and roots to eat. Or they just sit on top of their hills and look around.

Some prairie dogs are always on guard against danger to their town. If they see a snake or a coyote or a man on a horse, or if someone should pass in a car, they bark and shake. And quick as a flash all disappear.

Where do they go?

They dive into holes in the ground. The prairie dogs' towns are under the ground.

In making its home, a prairie dog digs with its paws. It digs straight down, deeper than the space between the floor and the ceiling of most houses—a long way to dig for a little animal not much bigger than a fat puppy.

At the bottom of the hole the prairie dog digs long hallways and then digs out the rooms where it will store food and where its babies will live.

The dirt from the hole has to go somewhere. So the prairie dog kicks it to the top of the hole and makes a hill around the entrance to its underground home.

These frisky little animals are fun to watch. They were a welcome sight to the early settlers of the American West. But after the settlers became ranchers, they no longer liked the prairie dogs because the little animals ate the grass that the ranchers wanted for their cattle. So millions of prairie dogs were killed, and soon almost none were left.

Just in time, the government set apart a hilltop park in Lubbock, Texas, and saved the biggest prairie-dog town in the Southwest. The prairie dogs have made Lubbock a famous place. People from many lands have come to see these friendly little creatures, which were once so much at home everywhere on the big prairies.

The Big Lizards

If you see a long, mossy-green log floating in the water, look carefully. It might not be a log. If you are in a hot, wet country, it might be a crocodile or an alligator.

Neither of these animals can breathe underwater, as a fish does, but each can hold its breath and swim underwater for a long time. Both have tough, thick skins to protect them from enemies, and a big mouthful of very sharp teeth.

Alligator

Crocodile

To many people a crocodile and an alligator look alike. But in some ways they are different, as the pictures show. Here is a rhyme about them:

While sailing down the river Nile,
I chanced upon a crocodile.
I knew him by his narrow nose,
His great long head, and scaly "clothes."

Far away and some time later,
I sailed up to an alligator.
Though shorter than the crocodile,
He seemed to stretch about a mile!

Now, both these reptiles swim with skill.
And both of them will bite and kill!
Both have teeth as sharp as nails,
Snapping jaws, and slapping tails.

They run quite fast on short, squat legs.
In sand and mud they lay their eggs.
And soon the small ones can be seen,
So tiny—but they grow up mean!

If you should ever have to go
Where these monsters live and grow,
I think you'd better watch them float
From the safety of a boat.

Danger! Sharks!

This man is taking photographs of the beautiful, bright-colored fish that live in the ocean. Suddenly, he sees a giant shape. It looks at first like a long, dark shadow.

The man doesn't wait to see any more because he knows that this big shadow thing is really a shark. And some sharks eat people!

Because some sharks are dangerous, a wire net is stretched along the shore, out in the water, at beaches where sharks have been seen. This keeps the sharks away and makes it safe to swim there. Many large beaches have been made safe for swimming.

Sharks aren't everywhere in the ocean, and not all sharks are man-eaters. But these great white sharks are. They are so fierce that fishermen call them tigers of the sea.

It's hard for a man to fight them because they are such strong, fast swimmers and have bodies that are protected by a tough skin covered with tiny, toothlike bones. In their big mouths are rows and rows of sharp teeth that rip like the edge of a saw. White sharks make a quick meal out of almost anything!

This is another man-eating shark. You may think he looks too funny to be dangerous, but he's really too dangerous to be funny.

He's called the hammerhead shark. If you hold the book sideways, you can see why.

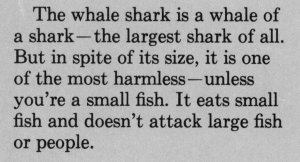

These small dogfish sharks can bite, but they are not likely to eat people. They are a big pest to a fisherman. The fish they don't eat, they scare away. Sometimes they even eat the fisherman's net.

It's only because they have faces that look a little like a dog's that they are named after man's friendliest pet.

The whale shark is a whale of a shark—the largest shark of all. But in spite of its size, it is one of the most harmless—unless you're a small fish. It eats small fish and doesn't attack large fish or people.

Some men work at catching sharks. They go hunting for them nearly every day. It is the way they make their money.

Just about every part of this big, dangerous fish is good for something.

The oil in a shark's liver contains vitamin A.

The skin of a shark makes a very tough leather
for belts and other things.

Some people collect shark teeth. You can find them in the sand on
many ocean shores. You can even make them into a necklace.

The meat of a shark is good to eat. But there are more sharks
caught than people want to eat, so some shark meat is made into
fertilizer. Farmers put fertilizer on their land to help things grow.

Even the fins of a shark are good for something. People in China
use them to make a soup.

Traveling on Water

The very first boat in the world . . .
What was it? A log?

That's a pretty good guess. A man could sit on a log and go floating down a river. If he paddled with his hands, he could make the log go a tiny, tiny bit faster. He could even turn it slowly.

But a log can flop and make you go plop. *Splash!* You're dripping wet.

Maybe one day someone tied three or four logs together with vines. This made something called a *raft*. A raft doesn't tip easily— but it moves no faster than a log, and it is hard to steer.

One day someone tried making a hollow place in a log where he could sit and where he could carry things. It seemed like a good idea, and other people started making these log boats. Sometimes the hollow place in the log was burned out with fire. Sometimes it was dug out with sharp sticks and stones.

People stopped using their hands for paddles. They used a flat stick instead. This made their log boat go faster.

Nobody knows who was first to put a sail on a boat. Maybe it was someone who saw a leaf being blown along on top of the water. We don't know what was used for the first sail. Maybe wide, tough leaves or woven grass. Maybe wide pieces of bark or bamboo. Whatever it was, people found that sailing was faster and easier than paddling.

Finally, someone built a ship that used a sail *and* long paddles, called *oars*. When there was no wind, the sailors rowed with the oars. When the wind blew in the same direction they were going, they put up the sail. Later, sailors learned to turn, or *set,* a sail to make the boat go in almost any direction they wished.

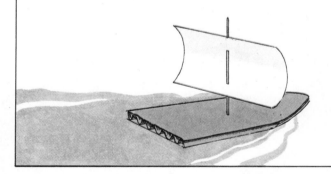

To see how the wind pushes a sailboat, make a sail out of a small piece of stiff paper and put a toothpick through it. Then push the toothpick into a cork or a piece of cardboard or a piece of bubbly foam plastic. Put it in a pan of water and blow on it. Pretend that your boat is sailing across the ocean.

When you stop blowing, what happens to your boat?

It stops, too. A sailboat goes only when the wind blows.

This big boat, with a sail and oars, was built long ago in the country of Greece.

People learned how to build sailing ships with masts so high they seemed to touch the sky. These ships had so many sails that oars were not needed.

After many years of sailing, people found a still better way to make boats move. They used paddles again, but this time they put the paddles in a wheel that was part of the boat. When the paddle wheel moved, the boat moved whether the wind blew or not.

Some of the paddle wheels were as big as a house! They were much too heavy to turn by hand. People had to use something new to make the paddle wheel turn.

They used steam. Steam turned an engine, and the engine turned the paddle wheel. Steamboats, with their tall chimneys puffing smoke and their steam whistles going *toot-toot,* sailed up and down the rivers and across lakes and oceans all over the world.

Today, there are many more kinds of engines that can make boats move. There are huge, fast ships with engines somewhat like those used in the big trucks that go roaring over the highways. Some boat engines even run with atomic power.

But all of the old kinds of boats are still used, too—sailboats, rowboats, canoes, and rafts.

Not very many people ride on a log anymore. But you still can if you want to.

How Did the Ship Get into the Bottle?

If you were a sailor on a ship, what would you do when you weren't working? Except when there's a storm, a sailor doesn't have to work all the time.

So what would you do? You could read or sleep. You could talk with your friends—if *they* weren't working. Or you could walk around the deck and look at the sky and ocean. But on a long, long trip you would probably get tired of these things.

Many sailors spend their spare time cutting, or *whittling,* things out of wood. Some sailors patiently carve small models of big things.

A sailor made this model of a ship and put it in the bottle.

Some people think that after the ship was made, it was taken to a bottle factory and that a bottle was made around the ship.

What do *you* think?

First, the sailor whittled out all the different parts of the ship. Then, carefully, he fitted each part to the next one.

He cut the sails out of cloth and fastened them to the big masts, and to the little masts, called *spars*.

Then he *rigged* the ship— fastened strings between all the masts and spars and sails to hold them in their proper places.

The masts and spars were too big to go into the bottle any way except endways. So he placed the masts right next to their holes and let them lie back flat on the ship's deck.

Then, so-o-o-o carefully, he slid everything endways into the bottle.

Now we're ready for the big trick.

Before the sailor slid the ship into the bottle, he tied a special long string to the masts and let the end of the string hang out.

With the ship snugly inside the bottle, he pulled the string and —presto—up came the masts and sails.

After the sailor cut the string off, there was no way to tell how the boat got into the bottle. It looked as if it had always been there.

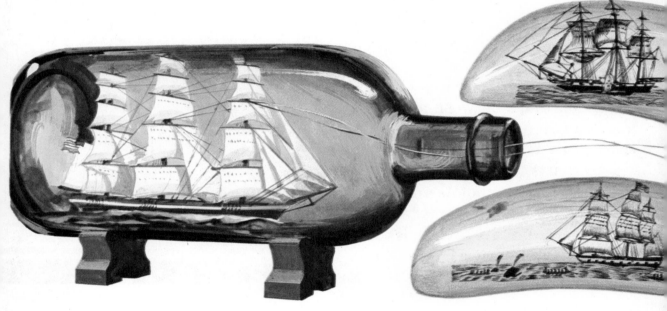

Sailors also used to carve pictures in their spare time. Here is one carved on a piece of ivory. Usually, the ivory came from the long, curved tooth of a walrus, called a *tusk*. Sometimes it came from an elephant's tusk. Sailors also carved pictures on shells and whales' teeth. These carvings were called *scrimshaw*. Why? Nobody knows. Maybe a sailor named Scrimshaw carved especially good ones.

The oldest carvings of ship models that we know about were made by the Egyptians—the same people who made the great stone pyramids. This is the model of an Egyptian ship carved from wood.

Far south in the ocean there are beautiful islands where palm trees and shining green plants grow. In the sun and the rain the plants grow fast and big. The people in these South Sea islands make toy boats for their children from the nuts and seeds dropped by these giant plants.

You can make models, too. You can make them out of almost anything—even folded pieces of paper. But it will take a lot of practice before you can make a big ship and put it inside a little bottle.

Hello, Snow

You are looking out the window of your warm house. The sky is colorless and cold. It looks as if it would ring and clang if you could raise your fist and knock on it. The wind blows. The sun is hiding. What an unfriendly day! You turn away from the window.

An hour later your mother says, "Come look out the window!"

You wonder what there is to see that wasn't there before. You wonder why it's so quiet. The sounds of the city—voices, engines, alarms, wheels, horns—are hushed. When you look out the window, you see why. It's snowing. The snow has made a brand-new world, clean and soft and silent.

As snowflakes fall from the sky, they look like feathers, bits of lace, silvery spider webs, chips from a diamond. . . .

It's easy to catch a snowflake, but keeping one is harder. Snowflakes melt so fast. Take a piece of black paper or cloth outside with you to catch and hold a few snowflakes. And take a magnifying glass to get a really good look.

At first glance all snowflakes look the same. That's because they all have six sides. A closer look will show you that they are not the same—every one is different.

Aren't they pretty? How would you like to have your room wallpapered with pictures of snowflakes? Every night when you went to bed, you could have your own private snowstorm.

Can you imagine snow almost every night? That's a lot of snow. But there are places where there is that much snow. Eskimos, who live far north, toward the bitterly cold North Pole, have that much snow. They have so much they can even make houses of it!

Even if it doesn't snow enough where you live to build a snow-house, perhaps there will be enough snow to make a fort or a snowman.

When it's very, very cold, the snow is as dry and unstickable as sand. It won't pack in your hands to make a snowball. But just wait until the sun comes out and softens the snow a little.

Then . . .

Look out, boys and girls! Here come the snowballs!

Snowballs come from boys and girls. Snowflakes come from the sky—from the billions of tiny water droplets up there that form clouds.

Sometimes the wind blows these clouds from a warm place to a very cold place. If the wind stops blowing, it leaves the clouds hanging in the freezing cold. When that happens, the tiny droplets of water in the cloud freeze into tiny ice crystals. And these ice crystals make up snowflakes.

Down
down
down
comes the downy snow.

The Animal That Plants Trees

Who argues with the blue jays,
jumps from one tip-top tree branch
to another tip-top tree branch,
and runs around with its cheeks
filled with nuts?
The squirrel, of course.

Can you see its parachute? And
its umbrella? Can you find the
extra blanket it's carrying?

Sure you can. Its parachute is its tail. When it makes long jumps from branch to branch, it uses its tail to slow itself down in the air and to help itself land on its feet if it falls from a high place.

Its tail is also its umbrella when it rains.

And when it's cold—well, it uses its tail for a blanket.

It even has other uses for its tail. The squirrel has many enemies, and it protects itself with its tail when it fights.

Chatter-chatter-chatter. Who's making all that noise?

A father squirrel is warning all the animals to stay away from his and mother squirrel's new babies sleeping in the nest. When they can't find a hollow tree, squirrels carry sticks and leaves and build nests in high tree branches. The father squirrel stays outside the nest, looking and listening and sniffing as he guards his family from animals that would like to steal his babies and eat them.

There are so many kinds of squirrels—gray squirrels, red squirrels, white squirrels, fox squirrels, ground squirrels, and flying squirrels. They are fun to watch and easy to tame. Watch them chase one another up and down tree trunks—along electric-light wires—up and down the sides of buildings—and over the rooftops. Watch them hide nuts and pinecones in hollow trees or dig holes and bury them under the ground.

Because they live most of their lives in trees, baby squirrels must learn such things as how to walk headfirst down a tree and

how to jump from one branch to another branch without falling. Then, someday, their mother will take them down the tree trunk and teach them how to find mushrooms and grasshoppers to eat without being caught by a hawk, a weasel, or a fox.

During the winter, when the ground is frozen or covered with snow, squirrels can eat the food they stored away. Nobody knows for sure how they find the nuts they bury. Maybe they smell them. Maybe they can see where the ground has been dug up a little. Squirrels in an oak or walnut forest bury so many nuts that it seems that they could dig almost anywhere and find an acorn or walnut.

Some of the hidden nuts are never found, and many grow to become trees. Squirrels are a great help in keeping our forests growing. They plant more trees than almost anybody.

A Tale About Tails

One of the most useful tools an animal has is its tail. Each kind of animal uses its tail for special things. Some animals hang by their tails from branches while gathering fruit.

An alligator uses its powerful tail to fight off enemies.

A fox uses its tail to keep warm. Other animals balance themselves with their tails as they

hop, 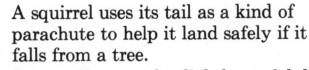 jump,

or fly.

A squirrel uses its tail as a kind of parachute to help it land safely if it falls from a tree.

Some tails are only slightly useful, like the cow's tail, which keeps pesky flies away.

Others are very useful.

The beaver uses its tail to sound a warning, to paddle and steer when it swims, to pack its home with mud, and to hold itself steady while it cuts a tree down with its teeth.

The beaver longed to have a tail
  not quite so short and flat.
The spider monkey swapped with him;
  it didn't stop with that!

The animals *all* joined the fun
  and swapped their tails around.
They thought a tail was just a tail,
  but this is what they found—

The beaver dangled overhead
  and gnawed the tree in two.
He felt quite silly when he fell;
  and why not—wouldn't you?

The monkey with a beaver's tail
  could never climb a tree.
So fruit and eggs were out of reach,
  while he watched—hungrily.

The robin with a squirrel's tail
  could hop but couldn't fly.
For feathers and not fluffy fur
  keep robins in the sky.

The lion took the robin's tail
  and put it to the test.
He tried to soar, gave one loud roar,
  and landed in a nest.

The skunk put on the lion's tail
  and carried it with pride.
The beasts all thought it was a joke
  and laughed until they cried.

The squirrel chose the skunk's fine tail,
    and when the air had cleared,
He tried to show it to his friends,
    but they had disappeared.

Some animals were hungry, cold,
    and some got scared and hid.
But in the end they worked it out—
    do you know what they did?

Each animal took back his tail,
    and, having done so, each
Had learned a simple lesson that
    mistakes can sometimes teach—

"The tail I took just couldn't seem
    to do as it was told.
And now I wouldn't swap my own
    for one made out of gold."

What Time Is It?

What is time?

Let's take time to think about it.

We talk about daytime, night-time, noon, and midnight.

Time for breakfast.

Time to go to bed.

Time to come in from playing.

Time to go to school. . . .

Time is also a time when your mother says, "Hurry or you'll be late."

Or when your father says, "Let's do that after dinner."

Time is *right now* and *before this* and *after that*.

When we want to tell time exactly, we use a watch or a clock. A watch or a clock is something that *measures* time. It tells us what time it is right now—what hour, what minute, what second.

The little hand on the watch or the clock tells us what hour it is. One o'clock . . . two o'clock . . . three o'clock . . .

We say, "At two o'clock my TV program comes on."

"At six o'clock my daddy comes home."

"Eight o'clock is my bedtime."

The big hand on the watch or the clock tells what minute it is between the hours. Sometimes a third hand tells what second. (A second is about as long as it takes you to say your name slowly or to take a deep breath.)

We can look at a clock, and if the clock says that it is five minutes until two o'clock, we know that in five minutes the TV program will start.

If we want to talk about yesterday or what week, what month or what year, then we have something else to measure time.

You know what that is.

A *calendar*.

How Does a Town Start?

First, there's a house where people live. Then another house . . . and another . . . and another. . . . Finally, there are so many that someone builds a store. And now people can buy things without having to bring them in from far away.

But that's not always how a town starts. Sometimes the store comes first. This is a story about one that did. It's a story that starts with the words "Once upon a time . . ." But it is a true story —a story that has happened in many places all over the world.

Once upon a time some men in a boat came up a river to explore wild country. The men were *traders*. They wanted to trade or sell things to the people in the wild country and buy things from them. The people who lived there could have been almost anybody, but these were Indians.

Day and night, day and night, the men in the boat kept moving up the river. Finally, they came to a place where another big river emptied into their river.

"Look," the leader said, "here where the two rivers meet—a good place to build our store. Plenty of trees that we can cut down to make our buildings. Land's high enough that we can fight off any enemies that attack. And the Indians can come to us from both rivers to sell things to us and to buy what we have to sell to them."

The men landed and cut down trees and built a log store, or *trading post*. They built some log houses to live in. And they built a strong fence around everything so that they would be safer if Indians attacked.

Some traders cheated the Indians. This made the Indians so angry that they sometimes attacked the traders with bows and arrows and tried to make them go away.

But let's say these traders didn't cheat the Indians, or not very much. So the Indians brought valuable furs to the trading post and traded them for guns and bullets, animal traps, and blankets and food. The men at the trading post sent the furs downriver to the big cities by the ocean and brought back more and more things to trade with the Indians for more and more furs—fox, coon, squirrel, skunk, bear, and especially beaver.

One day a man came and built a mill by the river to grind wheat and corn. Now the people who lived there could have fresh flour and cornmeal. Another man came who knew how to make leather from animal skins, and shoes for people and harnesses for horses. Another man came who knew how to fix broken guns and even make new ones. He also knew how to put iron shoes on horses. Someone else came who knew how to weave cloth and make clothes for people. And all the time, more people were coming and cutting down trees and starting gardens and farms.

Finally, there were enough people there at the place where the rivers met that they built a school, a church, and a post office . . . and later a man built a bank.

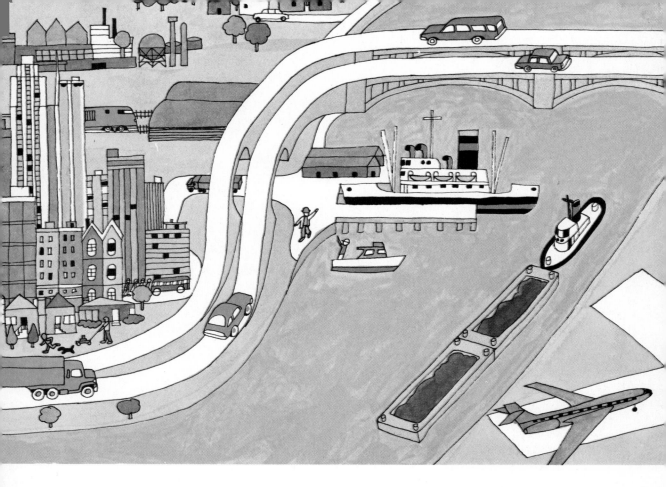

More and more boats were traveling on the river now. Even steamboats. Finally, a road was built through the woods all the way from the ocean to that town where the rivers met. Now big wagons came rolling, loaded with things for people to buy, and loaded with people who wanted to stay and live in that new country, which wasn't so wild anymore.

After steam engines were invented and people found out how to build railroad tracks, trains started coming to the town where the rivers met. And the town kept growing and growing.

The town is still there today, only now it is full of automobiles and factories and tall buildings. The town could be called Pittsburgh or St. Louis or Louisville or Omaha or any one of a lot of cities you have heard of and will surely visit someday.

Looking at Our Tall Friends

Peter made this drawing of a tree when he was four years old. How old were you when you drew your first tree? Did it look like Peter's? He made all the leaves look like a big green ball. Then he took a brown crayon and made a thick, straight line for a trunk.

Even though this is not an exact picture of a tree, you know right away what it is. Trees have a special look. They are very different from all the other plants on Earth. They stand up taller. They live longer. Some are the largest of all living things.

A few months later, Peter drew *this* tree. He drew it in the winter after the leaves had fallen to the ground. Now Peter could see the branches on the trees. He thought the branches looked like arms.

When you look at this picture, you know that Peter has learned something very important about trees. He has learned that trees have roots.

Often you can see some of the roots humping out of the ground from under the trunk of the tree. But there are many, many more roots that you can't see. The roots of a tree spread deep under the ground, just as its branches spread high across the sky. Roots hold a tree in the ground and keep it from falling over. They also keep the soil from blowing away.

Roots do something that is very important for a tree. They grow this way and that and find the water that is under the ground. They take up the water and send it up through the trunk and through the branches to the leaves.

A tree would die if it did not have roots under the ground, taking up water.

Peter has begun to see that not all trees look alike.

Some trees are very good for climbing because their branches start close to the ground. *(Sycamore)*

Others have trunks that stand taller than houses. Their branches don't even begin until the second floor. *(Aspen)*

There are trees that look like upside-down ice-cream cones. *(Spruce)*

Some trees look as trim as if they went to the barbershop every week. *(Sugar Maple)*

Sycamore

Spruce

Sugar Maple

Aspen

Peter sees that one kind of tree has one kind of leaf. Another kind of tree has another kind of leaf.

Some leaves are shaped like fans *(Ginkgo)*
    feathers *(Hickory)*
    stars *(Sweet Gum)*
    or mittens. *(Sassafras)*

Peter likes to draw trees because he feels that trees are his friends. They bring him cool shade. They hold out their branches like arms, inviting him to climb. When their leaves rub together, they seem to whisper secrets to him.

Trees are your friends, too. The more you look at them, the more you'll find out about them. And, as you grow older, you will find more and more reasons to be glad there are trees.

Ginkgo

Hickory

Sweet Gum

Sassafras

Before There Were Wheels

Wheels,

wheels,

wheels . . .

Big wheels, little wheels,

wide wheels, thin wheels.

Iron wheels, brass wheels,

and big rubber-tired wheels.

Wheels of wood and wheels of plastic.

Every kind of wheel you can think of—

even toy wheels and candy wheels.

Can you imagine if there weren't any—no wheels anywhere in the world?

Without wheels many of your toys couldn't move. Your wagon. Your tricycle. Your roller skates.

Without the wheels that go around and around in a factory machine, we couldn't make books or tin cans or any of the other things that are made by machine.

A motorboat couldn't run without the wheels in its engine. An airplane couldn't get off the ground or get safely down again. And a train couldn't run.

Before there were wheels, people did not go very far very fast.

People carried things on their backs or heads or dragged things behind them.

It might be fun to travel this way. But you could go no faster than your bearers could walk.

After animals were tamed, things were carried on the backs of camels, llamas, horses, elephants, oxen, and donkeys.

Sometimes two poles were attached to the sides of a horse or even a dog. The poles dragged in the dirt behind the walking animal and held the weight of whatever was being moved.

We don't know who was the first one in the world to use a wheel. Perhaps someone watched a log roll down a hill and thought, "What a good way to move something heavy—on top of a rolling log!"

It wasn't a very good way, though. Things kept falling off.

People tried using more than one log and rolling the logs along together. It was hard, slow work, but very heavy weights could be moved in this way.

Try moving a small box—or a brick—in this way—
Use a few pencils to carry the weight. Just keep picking up the leftover pencil and placing it in front of the box as you push it along.

And then . . .
Perhaps one day someone cut the end from a log and made the first wheel!

A wheel rolling by itself can't carry anything. The wheel must be attached to something.

The wheel has to be put on a rod called an *axle*. Then the wheel can turn on the axle and make something move. After people found out how to attach a wheel to an axle and attach the axle to a cart or wagon and later to a wheelbarrow or bicycle or train or anything else, life became easier for them.

Today we use so many wheels that it is hard to imagine how people ever got along without them.

You can try it yourself and see how it works. Cut some wheels from stiff paper or cardboard.

Push a pencil through the center of one of the wheels. The pencil is your axle. Wiggle the pencil in the paper to make the hole big enough so that your wheel turns on your pencil axle.

Before you put a wheel on the other end of your axle, bend up the two sides of a piece of cardboard. Push the pencil through the two sides.

Do the same thing with two other wheels and another pencil axle. Now you have a wagon!

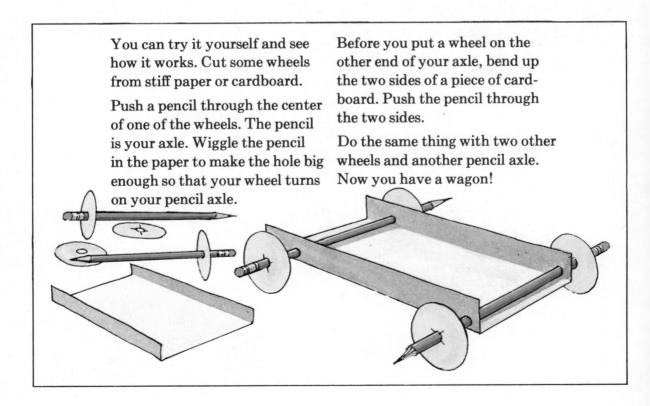

Wheels, wheels, wheels . . .

Can you tell what each of these wheels is?

(The answers are printed upside down at the bottom of the page.)

1. automobile wheel. 2. airplane wheel. 3. tractor wheel. 4. bicycle wheel. 5. cogwheel of clockworks. 6. a child's hoop. 7. roller skate wheel. 8. caster wheel. 9. flanged railroad wheel. 10. Ferris wheel. 11. steering wheel. 12. tricycle wheel. 13. coaster wagon wheel.

How Do You Tell a Storybook Wolf

Let's look at what the storybook wolf did in the story of Little Red Riding Hood.

Remember the story? Little Red Riding Hood was taking a basket of food to her grandmother who lay sick in bed in her little house deep in the woods. On her way, Little Red Riding Hood met a wolf who asked her where she was going.

Now Little Red Riding Hood's mother had told her not to talk to anybody along the way. But she forgot and told the wolf where her grandmother lived and that she was sick in bed. . . .

from a Real Wolf?

    You don't have to know much about wolves to know that they do not speak or understand words.

    But do you know that wolves can't make plans the way people do? Wolves don't say to themselves, "First I will do this. Then I will do that. And then I will do that." Wolves don't seem to think very much about anything. They do feel many things—hunger, cold, fear. . . .

    The minute wolves feel one of these things, they usually do something about it. A hungry, real wolf that met a little girl alone in the woods might eat her right on the spot!

When the wolf heard that Little Red Riding Hood's grandmother lay sick and helpless in bed, he ran ahead as fast as he
could to her house. He tied up Little Red Riding Hood's grandmother and locked her in the closet. Then he pushed a nightcap
down over his ears and crawled into bed. . . .

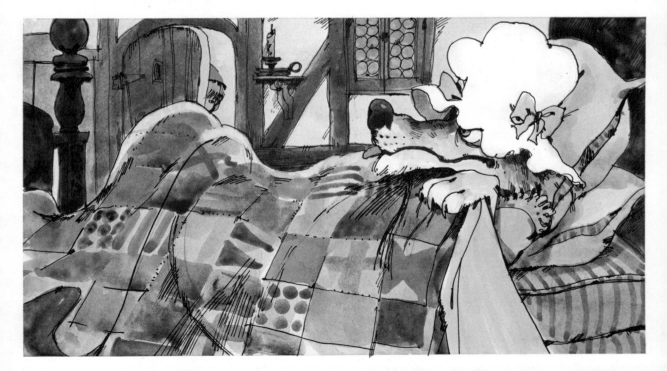

No real wolf puts on people's clothing to fool the creatures it is trying to catch. But the color of some wolves at different times of the year protects them from enemies and helps them sneak up and catch the animals they eat.

In spring and summer, when baby wolves are born, the fur of the wolf is reddish brown. This is the color of the ditches and shallow open caves where a wolf family makes its home.

In winter, the coat of a wolf turns yellowish brown like the dead leaves and weeds in the woods where it lives.

The fur of the Far North wolf turns snowy white, and darkens only after the long winter is over.

Little Red Riding Hood went right into her grandmother's bedroom and sat down beside the bed.

"How nice to see you, my dear," said the storybook wolf, trying to make his gruff voice as sweet as the grandmother's.

Little Red Riding Hood looked at her grandmother's bedcap, which the wolf's stiff ears kept poking up higher and higher. "What big ears you have," she said.

"The better to hear you with, my dear," said the wolf.

Then Little Red Riding Hood looked at her grandmother's eyes. "What big eyes you have, Grandmother."

"The better to see you with, my dear," said the wolf, smiling.

Little Red Riding Hood looked at her grandmother's smile. "And what big teeth you have, Grandmother!"

"The better to eat you with!" cried the wolf, jumping out of bed.

When Little Red Riding Hood heard *that*, she turned and ran. She ran until she came to some woodchoppers who were working in the forest. When she told them what had happened, they went back to the little house and killed the wolf with their axes. . . .

Most wolves can run faster than foxes and even deer. So a real wolf could easily have caught Little Red Riding Hood.

But the storybook wolf and the real wolf are alike in one way. They both want to eat living things. Real wolves can't live on grass and leaves and the roots of plants as some animals do. They have to eat meat. If they don't, they get sick and die. This is the way wolves are. It is not because wolves are mean or bad or wicked.

A hundred years ago, there were more wolves than wolf food. There just weren't enough wild animals for the wolves to kill and eat. Hungry wolves came out from their natural homes—the deep forests—and killed farm animals, such as sheep and cows and horses. So the farmers started killing the wolves. They killed so many that now there are not many wolves left.

But wolves are still bad in most stories. It doesn't hurt their feelings, though. That's because wolves can't read. (You don't have to know much about wolves to know that.)

Printed in the United States of America